WICKETKEEPING

A COMPREHENSIVE MODERN GUIDE

FOR PLAYERS AND COACHES

WICKETKEEPING

A COMPREHENSIVE MODERN GUIDE

FOR PLAYERS AND COACHES

JAMES KNOTT & ANDREW O'CONNOR

FOREWORD BY
ALEC STEWART

With contributions from
Jack Russell, Alan Knott, David Ripley,
Ben Duckett, Tom & Peter Moores

This edition first published in 2021 by

POLARIS PUBLISHING LTD
c/o Aberdein Considine
2nd Floor, Elder House
Multrees Walk
Edinburgh
EH1 3DX

Distributed by
Birlinn Limited

www.polarispublishing.com

ISBN: 9781913538316
eBook ISBN: 9781913538323

British Library Cataloguing-in-Publication Data
A catalogue record for this book is available on request from the British Library.

Designed and typeset by Polaris Publishing, Edinburgh
Printed in Great Britain by MBM Print, East Kilbride

CONTENTS

FOREWORD

If there is one thing about wicketkeeping that sets it apart from other specialist roles in cricket, it is that it can be a lonely business. Batters and bowlers always have company. As a keeper you are very often left on your own and because you wear gloves everyone assumes you will catch every ball that comes your way. I can promise you it is not as easy as that!

Some would also argue that the pure art of keeping wicket is a lost one. The most natural keepers no longer come to the fore as a greater onus is placed upon runs produced than chances taken behind the stumps. The modern game demands that a balance is struck between the two and at times it would be fair to suggest it is now weighted too greatly towards the batting side of the equation.

There is no debate that I was a batsman who became a wicketkeeper and that my keeping improved the longer I did it for. The fact is that I only really began learning to keep wicket while playing for England. It sounds ridiculous but it is true. Due to the presence of an England international wicketkeeper in Jack Richards when I came through at Surrey, there was no reason for me to devote too much time to my keeping as my way into the first team would be as a top-order batsman. I kept wicket each winter for Midland-Guildford CC in Perth Grade cricket in Australia before making my England debut as I realised early on in my career how valuable it would be to have another string to my bow and I always had a huge desire to get better as a cricketer in whatever way I could.

The brilliant Alan Knott, the father of the co-author of this book, helped me tremendously while he was wicketkeeping coach to the England team during the 1990s. He deserves huge credit for helping me get to the point where at the start of the international winter of 1996-97 I was told I would be the first-choice keeper.

I also gained a great deal from training with, listening to and watching the man who wore the gloves when I first started with England, my great mate Jack Russell – exactly how he practised and what went into his preparation. Like any top batter or bowler, things always look slightly different when they are done by the very best. The ball melts into the gloves of a high-class keeper.

I played with and against some top-class wicketkeepers during my first-class career spanning 22 years. In addition to Russell, who was the best English keeper I played with, the other man who stood out for me was Keith Piper of Warwickshire. I maintain he was the best keeper not to win an England cap. His glovework was exceptional, both stood back to the extreme pace of Allan Donald or up to the stumps, and he arguably suffered when it came to higher honours for being one of those pure glovemen whose batting was not quite good enough.

The skill of standing up to the seamers in limited-overs cricket was an essential part of the wicketkeeper's job in the 80s and 90s and it is arguably no coincidence that the teams of Russell and Piper – Gloucestershire and Warwickshire – were so successful. Moments of brilliance, like leg-side stumpings, would often prove to be match-defining ones.

That work up to the stumps arguably sets the very best apart from the very good, and Ian Healy is a case in point. He was the number-one wicketkeeper I came up against in international cricket. His work to Shane Warne in particular, reacting to those huge leg breaks, especially when Warne bowled around the wicket into the rough, and reading the variations was outstanding.

As people have become used to more runs, scored more quickly, across all formats, there are fewer out-and-out keepers these days – you have to be looked upon as an all-rounder now, so the way you bat and the runs you score are crucial. James Foster, as pure a gloveman as you could wish to see, would be the one keeper in recent times to have missed out on a vast number of England Test caps due to the selectors picking superior batsmen-keepers ahead of him. Ben Foakes, the 67th man handed the gloves by England in Test cricket, is currently the best gloveman in the world in my opinion and he has shown he can bat at the highest level too when posting a hundred on his Test debut. Despite this, the England selectors are currently picking perceived better batsmen-keepers ahead of him. Foakes, who I have the pleasure of working with at Surrey, is a genuine all-rounder in the modern game and I hope his artistry with the gloves along with his talent with bat in hand will be seen on the international stage for a long time.

And that, I guess, as this book shows, is the goal for all aspiring wicketkeepers of today – master the art of keeping wicket and make sure you can bat too.

Alec Stewart
Surrey & England

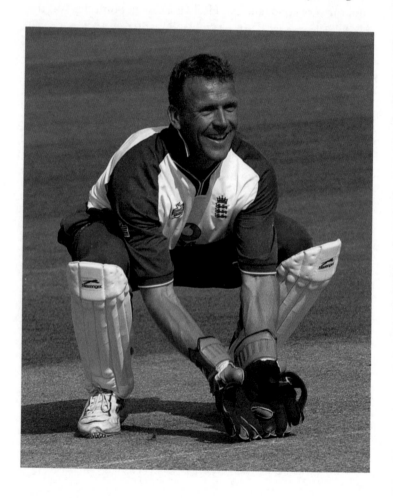

INTRODUCTION

The wicketkeeper is central to any cricket team and is a very exciting role for any player to have. You are constantly in the game and vital to the team, whether it is initiating catches and stumpings, changing the course of the game with a special dismissal, energising the team, advising the captain and bowler, limiting extras, tidying up poor throws, or offering words of encouragement to your team-mates. Moreover, you are possibly batting in the top order and scoring vital runs.

This book is aimed at all wicketkeepers, wherever you are on your wicketkeeping journey, be that a beginner or a seasoned professional. If you are thinking about trying wicketkeeping for the first time, then please consider these words from Ben Duckett (Nottinghamshire & England):

I think it's so important at a young age to give everything a go because you never know how good you will be. Wicketkeeping is a great chance to get involved in the game if you're not a bowler. Therefore, it takes the pressure off your batting, as you can contribute whilst keeping too.

This book is also for all cricket coaches, whether they have personal wicketkeeping experience or not. It gives comprehensive guidance on the technical, tactical, physical, mental, lifestyle and training elements of wicketkeeping. Many cricket coaches who do not have experience of keeping themselves may be lacking in confidence, so are reluctant to tackle this discipline in any depth. However, there are many similar fundamental principles that are transferable from batting:

- A solid base in set-up to achieve a balanced position
- A still head position as the bowler releases the ball and as the batter executes their shot
- Watching the ball
- Decision-making
- Quick movement whilst still tracking the ball
- A need to let the ball come (in most cases), and the timing of the taking of the ball, as opposed to hitting it
- A relaxed body and an alert mind
- The ability to concentrate for long periods of time

These principles are detailed throughout the book, aiming to give the coach the confidence to drive forward with their wicketkeeping coaching.

As with any aspect of cricket there are several ways of achieving the same thing, and there are so many different styles out there. We will provide various options on how to set up, how to take the ball, diving techniques, leg-side takes, etc. Look at any of the current international cricketers out there and no two are the same. Hopefully, from the various methods suggested, you will find what works for you. Ultimately, you need to understand your own game and play to your strengths.

As coaches we also need to thoroughly know the players we work with and be open-minded enough to come out of our comfort zones and try new things. What may work for one player may not necessarily work for another. We hope this book gets you thinking confidently enough to adapt and add to its content, specifically for the individual keepers you work with. There are many contributions from current players and coaches, as well as former greats dotted throughout this book, and there is a comprehensive drills section in Chapter 9, which will help to keep training fun and varied.

Ultimately, we hope everyone who reads this book will be enlightened and inspired by it, arousing a curiosity for the beautiful and extremely enjoyable art of wicketkeeping.

Note for players and coaches
Remember, whatever level you are currently playing or coaching, you can always learn something new. Learn from watching videos of the best players, learn from the players and coaches you play with and against, and always strive to be better tomorrow than you are today.

Throughout this book, all technical descriptions and drill references are for keeping wicket to a right-hand batter unless stated otherwise.

ONE
THE BASICS

The key basics for wicketkeepers are to stay relaxed and watch the ball. Try and get your head in line with the ball whenever possible. The closer your head is to your hands in general, the more chance you have of catching the ball.

PETER MOORES

Nottinghamshire Head Coach and former England Head Coach

We did not like calling this chapter 'The Basics', as it implies easy or simple. However, as with any other discipline within the game, it is the basics that need to be mastered first before progressing further. Consistent success is usually achieved by the basics being executed really well over a long period of time. There is little point in pulling off a blinding one-handed catch, only to drop two that come straight at you, or letting several byes through. It is essential that you are proficient at the basics.

So, we have established that there are many principles for wicketkeeping that are similar to those for batting. The one we are going to explore first is the need for a solid base.

Footwork and balance are the most important aspects of wicketkeeping stood back to the fast bowlers. You need to get your head into line with the ball, and balance is key to be able to move quickly from side to side.

DAVID RIPLEY

Northamptonshire Head Coach & London Spirit Assistant Coach

Set-up and achieving a solid base

As with batting, a solid base is so important for two main reasons: it provides a still head position (which is crucial as the bowler releases the ball), and a powerful position from which to move quickly. As the bowler lets go of the ball, a wicketkeeper needs to be still. What you do prior to this is not that important. Some wicketkeepers have a trigger movement, others do not (more on that later). As long as you are still upon the bowler's ball release, you will be in a strong position that enables quick movement.

Wicketkeepers always used to be encouraged to adopt the following stance as the bowler ran in:

However, this position is not a good one to move quickly from. A much more dynamic position is this:

We will call this the 'ready' or 'set' position. Legs are wider than shoulder-width apart and the knees are bent, weight is predominantly on the balls of the feet and equally loaded on each leg. This is sometimes called the 'Z' position, a term that has been used for the correlation of the lower leg, upper leg and back orientation. It ensures a posture that provides stability, power, control and good head position.

The important thing here is to have a good 'power' position, with the knees bent and the back straight. This puts the keeper in a position where they can move powerfully from the stance, whilst ensuring they are protecting their back from strain and injury. A good way of remembering this shape is to think 'chin up, backside out'. Importantly, the head is still and the eyes level. The player looks comfortable and in a position to move quickly. Take a look at Jos Buttler's ready position on delivery for a good example.

This is why most modern keepers do not go down into the traditional stance when they are stood back to the faster bowlers – because they only have to get up again before the bowler delivers the ball. Stances do vary from standing up to the wicket to standing back, and these are discussed in more detail in later chapters.

In terms of hand position, at this point it is really down to personal preference. Some wicketkeepers will have their hands together, others apart.

Note for coaches

If a player has had an issue with not getting their hands together in time to take the ball, then together in the ready position probably serves best. However, hands apart can allow a more naturally dynamic position to move quickly, especially if there is a necessity to dive. If apart, it is important that both hands are in a similar position to help maintain balance and even weight distribution on each leg. Keepers should not load weight on one side or the other, as this will adversely affect their ability to move in the desired direction. Again, this is similar to batting. Batters that load too much on their front or

---

back foot will improve moving in one direction but will find it detrimental when needing to move on to the opposite foot.

Trigger movements or pre-delivery movements

At this point we should give some detail on trigger movements. As with batting, players can find these very useful as part of their pre-delivery routine. Similar to batters, wicketkeepers can find this beneficial for getting the feet moving and attaining the ready position for each delivery, whatever comes down, whether the ball is edged, missed, left or hit by the batter. Some wicketkeepers do stand very still – simply in a good ready position – but most need a pre-delivery routine to feel ready to move. It can also form part of the switching-on routine 'mentally' for each delivery, ensuring the player is ready for action. We discuss mental alertness and concentration in more depth in Chapter 6.

Pre-delivery movements can take many forms. If you are a proponent of the traditional stance, then your trigger will simply be standing up and planting your feet into the ready position. Others like to walk in with the bowler as they near the end of their run-up, similar to a fielder, and then adopt the ready position. This can be by stepping into that position or jumping in. Whatever your preference, it has to be the same and your weight needs to be evenly distributed on each leg.

Similar to batting, the crucial elements of a trigger movement are the timing of them to achieve a still, solid base as the bowler releases the ball, and that they are well ingrained and consistently repeatable for every delivery. Once a favoured routine is established, it is important to practise it so it becomes second nature and is exactly the same for each delivery. Your pre-delivery movement will almost certainly differ whether you are stood up to the wicket or stood back. Stood up, coming up with the ball is vital, but is not as important when stood back, where the ability to be able to cover larger distances is required more often.

Trigger movements are discussed in more detail in the chapters specifically discussing standing back or standing up to the wicket. Do have a look at Jos Buttler keeping wicket to see a good example of a simple and controlled trigger movement from a traditional stance.

Note for coaches

Where possible, film your wicketkeepers in action, both in training and matches. This is a powerful tool to not only highlight areas of improvement, but as an important record of the times when your wicketkeeper played well, so you can refer back to this footage if there is a period when they are not performing as well. At these times it often goes right back to the basics. A really good phone app is Cricket Coach Plus HD, which allows good slow-motion and frame-by-frame replays.

Watching the ball

*Hand-eye co-ordination is everything, so practise
catching until it becomes second nature.*

JACK RUSSELL

Gloucestershire & England

Again similar to batting, watching the ball is a crucial aspect of catching the ball cleanly on a consistent basis. If a solid base has been achieved, your head will be still and eyes level, giving you the best chance of picking up the ball early, enabling you to determine length and line, and any movement likely in the air. The earlier you can ascertain this information, the quicker you will move into a position to take the ball should it come through to you. If you are only picking up the ball halfway down its flight, your reaction and subsequent movements will be slower than if you pick it up as it leaves the bowler's hand.

You will also find it useful if you can start tracking the ball in the hand like a batter would, identifying different grips for variations and changes of pace. Keeping wicket to the same bowler regularly will enable you to develop a knowledge of what they are about to bowl before they deliver the ball, and perhaps even whilst they are still running in!

Next time you are keeping to a bowler, as they run in, see if you can spot on which side they are presenting the shiny side of the ball and the angle of the seam.

One question asked regularly is whether a wicketkeeper should watch the ball all the way into the gloves. This largely depends on where the player's starting point for taking a catch is. Someone like Jos Buttler likes to take the ball in front of his body, then step to the side to take to the left side of his body. His head tracks the ball all the way.

If a wicketkeeper prefers to catch the ball closer to their body and 'give' into their body, it is harder to track the ball with the eyes all the way in, as to do so the body will need to 'slump' so the head moves over the ball. Here it is advisable for a keeper to keep their head up and watch the ball as far as they can into the gloves. Sarfaraz Ahmed is a good example of someone who takes the ball this way.

If a ball swings after pitching or starts to 'wobble' in multiple directions, laterally and vertically, then attempting to watch the ball all the way into the gloves is crucial. Where it is physically possible to do so, the keeper should stay in line with the ball and give to the body.

Stood up to the wicket, we always encourage a wicketkeeper to watch the ball into the gloves, as so many stumpings are missed when a player prematurely attempts the stumping before taking the ball, being visually distracted by the position of the stumps or the location of the batter's feet. Drilling yourself to watch the ball all the way into your hands will make sure it is cleanly taken before going for the stumps. Remember to want and expect to take every single ball bowled and every single ball thrown in from the outfield.

In the next three chapters we discuss in more detail the various methods of taking the ball stood back and stood up to the wicket, and there is a comprehensive set of drills in Chapter 9 that can improve hand-eye co-ordination and your ability to track the ball.

Catching the ball

The most important basic to nail down on wicketkeeping is catching the ball. You need to present a big catching area, with thumbs out, elbows in and presenting the palms not the fingers to the ball. If you're not catching many balls, you're not going to enjoy it!
DAVID RIPLEY

Ultimately, the role of the wicketkeeper is to catch the ball repeatedly, and if you can do this consistently, you cannot ask any more of yourself. A strong ready position base will help your head position and your ability to watch and track the ball into the gloves. A good catching technique and the timing of taking the ball will mean you take the ball consistently, whether there is movement in the air, off the pitch, from the edge of the bat or if it has simply come straight through.

As previously mentioned, wicketkeepers vary on whether they keep their hands together or apart in their set-up. Some find starting with them together helps to keep their gloves together when taking the catch. Others prefer hands apart, as it is more natural. Slip fielders also vary on this. Some even stand with their hands on their knees right up to the moment the bowler delivers.

Whichever method you prefer, the timing of the take is crucial and there nearly always needs to be some give, particularly to the faster bowlers, whether stood up or back. One point that may influence your decision-making on this is that bowlers often use the keeper's gloves as a point of reference, and they generally like to see hands together and a nice big catching area!

Generally, most balls you catch will be with the fingers pointing to the ground, the orthodox take. The sweet spot we are aiming for here is the palm of the hand just below the little finger and third finger.

You will see from the image that the hands are overlapped slightly, little fingers crossed, and that the ball should be taken in your more dominant hand. Try to present as big a catching area as possible, with thumbs out, keeping arms and hands relaxed so that your hands give slightly on taking the ball, closing around the ball as you complete the take. Whilst the thumbs are to be out, it is essential they are loose and relaxed. Lay a wicketkeeping glove on the floor face up and you will see that the thumb has been made to stay in a wide, naturally relaxed position.

To allow give it is important that your arms and hands are relaxed, whether you are stood up or stood back to the wicket. Bent elbows will enable you to achieve this. Try this experiment: with your arms out straight and elbows locked tight, does that feel like a comfortable, relaxed position? Relax instead and bend your elbows, bringing your hands together. This should feel more natural and allow the right amount of give upon taking the ball. This can be into your body or to the side. Some keepers like to imagine the feel of heavy shoulders. By doing this they feel that their arms are looser and more relaxed to give with the ball. In this position, the fingertips will generally always point towards the floor upon taking a normal height delivery.

It is not just important to have relaxed elbows, but also that the elbows are not out away from the body. Elbows out forces the hands apart at the palms, and it can be difficult to get them back together in time to effect the catch correctly.

Note for coaches

If a player is wearing dark-coloured clothing and their glove face is light coloured, it is easy to see a dark inverted triangle appear between their hands if the palms have moved apart.

*Time the catch to perfection – know the exact moment the ball
will meet your gloves. Don't just catch the ball – swallow it.*

ALAN KNOTT

Kent & England

If you become an expert at catching the ball in the sweet spot
often enough, even with good timing and give, you may start to
develop bruising on the padded area just below your third finger
and little finger. This is a good sign that you are catching the ball
correctly. However, if it becomes an issue you may want to adjust
the area slightly to a firmer part of your hand that has more natural
protection as in this photo:

If you practise catching the ball in this area enough, it will start to feel natural, and it also has the benefit of protecting your fingers. They can take a pounding over the course of a full season, and it is very rare to find a keeper who has not broken a finger at some stage. However, if you become a master at catching the ball in the lower part of the palm, you will have a lot fewer finger-related issues.

For balls coming above shoulder height, more wicketkeepers now reverse their hands, fingers pointed up vertically. The sweet spot now relocates to below the first and second fingers.

Again, stay relaxed with elbows bent and give to the side of your head. There is no real alternative to giving to the side of your head or above it, as it is important for safety and for watching the ball that your head remains off-line. If a ball is coming towards your head and you put your hands up to catch it, you will lose sight of the ball, which greatly reduces your chances of taking it cleanly. And if you have mistimed the take, you could also get hit in the face!

Some keepers do not always use reverse hands when the ball goes above shoulder height. Quinton de Kock often prefers a more traditional take and rotates his body to enable him to get his hands above his head. Conversely, some wicketkeepers prefer a reverse-hands take. Jonny Bairstow (Yorkshire & England) often bends a lot at the knees so that he can take chest-high balls with reverse hands.

On a typical English early-season wicket, you will often be taking the ball low to the ground. No matter how close you stand, the ball rarely gets waist high or above. Here, the hands position is orthodox, and you can give between your legs, or move your legs out of the way and give to the side of them. You can also go into a long barrier-style position to get you low to take these deliveries. This also offers a good position if the ball does not carry, as you have a large body surface area to stop the ball if taking it cleanly is not possible.

For takes to the side of the body it is important, where possible, not to have straight arms, and to not take your head away from the line of the ball. Instead, move your body to get your head closer to the ball and tuck the lower of your elbows into your body to produce a wider catching area, as shown here:

You will also see in this photo that the hips have rotated to allow a 'giving' area. For takes to the side, aim to take in line with your head and give behind your head line. An alternative to this is discussed later, but this is a good starting point.

One-handed catching

*Most keepers can catch the easy balls, but the
best keepers catch all the difficult balls too.*
JACK RUSSELL

One-handed catching is often not coached enough. There are theories that you can use your feet to get to the ball two-handed all of the time, so one-handed catching is simply not necessary. It is true that you will not be required to take many balls one-handed in a game. However, when the opportunity arises it will be very important to catch the ball as it is quite likely to have come from the edge of the bat and to be a wicket-taking opportunity for the team. If you have not taken too many one-handed catches in your career, then it could be for one of two reasons: you are not practising it enough, so when the opportunity comes you put it down; or you are simply not going for them, probably because you have not practised them enough, and you are not confident to go for them in the first place!

The sweet spot for a one-handed take is the same as the reverse-hands technique: below the first and second fingers. To practise one-handed catching, take balls that you would normally take two-handed to the side of your body with one hand only. Keep elbows relaxed. Take in line with your head and give behind. Keep the give to a minimum, just enough to cushion the catch. Keep your head still, following the ball all the way into the glove. Most importantly, keep your hand on the line of the ball for as long as possible – avoid flicking out.

One-handed diving takes are discussed in more detail in the next chapter.

It is important that you practise these basics regularly. Any practice should incorporate a trigger movement if you have one in a game, and, in practice, always exaggerate the technical points so they are thoroughly ingrained.

Pre-match preparation is discussed in Chapter 8, but a really good pre-match routine is to do a minimum of ten of all of these takes in the time leading up to the match starting:

- 10 low catches
- 10 orthodox catches
- 10 shoulder height and above
- 10 either side of the body
- 10 one-handed catches – both hands
- 10 diving catches – both sides (one- and two-handed)

Note for coaches

Why not ask the wicketkeeper to rate their take on a scale of one to ten for each one. If it is perfectly in the sweet spot with the right amount of give, it is a ten! If it flicks a finger or thumb on the way in, they take some points off. If it is more in their fingers or webbing, do the same. Equally, if their hands were too hard/tense, or they do not give enough, they score lower. With regular practice they will be achieving tens on a regular basis.

Wicketkeeping in different countries

The general cricket wickets of the nine Test-playing nations around the world have different characteristics. Temperature, rainfall, humidity, geographical location, soil type, pitch preparation, etc., all have an influence on how a wicket will play. Types of ball and the age of the ball also have an influence on the play, as does general wear and tear on the pitch during play. In response to this, a wicketkeeper will face different technical, tactical, physical and mental challenges, depending upon where they are playing. They could be keeping on a very fast, bouncy pitch, or a slow, low-bouncing one with great spin. The list below gives a very general indication of how wickets play in these countries.

UK and New Zealand
Wickets here are generally fairly similar, with more grass than other countries. There is less pace and bounce, as the wickets are not as hard as in some countries, but the ball swings and seams around much more. There is also less spin here. The countries are similar, both in climate and geographical conditions, but an English summer can almost go through three seasons, so the wickets can change during that period. In the UK, the Readers and Dukes balls tend to swing more. In New Zealand, Kookaburra balls are used.

India, Pakistan, Sri Lanka and Bangladesh
There is hardly any live grass on these wickets, if any at all. There is less bounce and not much pace, but the wickets are hard and quite skiddy for opening bowlers. The ball spins much more

here than in any of the other countries, with bounce for the spinners. The wickets are dry and dusty, so the ball deteriorates fairly quickly. Also, the wickets themselves produce cracks and crumble, encouraging spin bowling. The ball can reverse swing regularly here. India use SG balls, whilst Pakistan, Sri Lanka and Bangladesh use the Kookaburra.

West Indies

Because the temperatures here are generally hot all year, the wickets are usually very hard and quick, with very good bounce and carry. There is little or no grass on them. The ball does not seam or swing very much at all. There is very little turn for the spinners, but there is bounce. There was a period when the wickets here were prepared to be very slow and low-bouncing, but they are now once again fast and bouncy. Dukes balls are used here regularly.

South Africa

As in the West Indies, it is generally warm here, so the wickets tend to be hard and quick, giving good bounce and carry. There is little live grass on the wickets, but the ball seams around less than in the UK but more than Australia. The ball does swing around whilst fairly new. It does not spin that much normally but does bounce. Kookaburra balls are used, which generally do not swing as much as the balls used in the UK.

Australia

Once again, the temperatures here are generally hot all year, so the wickets are very hard and quick, with very good bounce and carry. There is little live grass on the wickets, and the ball does not seam or swing around too much. The ball does spin a bit and does bounce. Kookaburra balls are used here too, which generally do not swing as much as the balls used in the UK.

The wickets in each of these countries display different challenges for the wicketkeeper to contend with, but hopefully the contents of this book will allow them to meet those challenges confidently and with great success.

TWO
STOOD BACK TO SEAM BOWLING

*Footwork and balance are the two most important aspects of standing back
to fast bowling. You need to get your head into line with the ball, and
balance is the key to being able to move quickly from side to side.*

DAVID RIPLEY

*When keeping to Stuart Broad I always feel I am in the game and I need to stay
relaxed and trust my instinct – mentally alert for a chance every ball, which could be
an outside or inside edge because he moves the ball late.*

TOM MOORES

Nottinghamshire 1st XI wicketkeeper

Where to stand

The general rule of thumb for judging how far back to stand
is to be taking the ball as it just starts to drop, and that will
vary depending on the pace of the bowler, combined with the
pace and bounce in the pitch. The age of the match ball can
also influence your distance back from the stumps. An old ball
means you may be closer than you would be with a new ball. A
fast bowler at the start of their spell may bowl slightly slower as
they get warmed up than when they are fully warmed up, so this
will also influence the stood-back position.

This distance can vary match by match and can also depend
on the level you are playing at. Even if a wicket is not bouncing
above knee height, the distance to go back is still just as the ball

starts to drop. This is to allow enough time to react if the batter edges the ball. Too close and you will not have time to react; too far back and the ball may not carry. A comfortable catching height is to take the ball between waist and knee height.

Within the first few deliveries of a bowler's spell, you can determine the correct distance, and if you keep to someone regularly you will have a good idea of your starting point. Occasionally, you will encounter a wicket that has so much bounce that the ball is often still rising as it gets to you, but there will still be a point where the pace of the ball reduces enough that it starts to drop, even if that is at head height.

For your initial positioning, in terms of line, a good starting point is for your left foot to be in line with off stump. Even if a batter has a bat swing that heads out towards gully, you should still have a clear view of the bowler running in and releasing the ball. As explained in the previous chapter, the view of the release point is vital to gain the information you need to judge where the ball is likely to be upon reaching you.

There is an argument that a wicketkeeper should have a starting point wider than off stump, as this allows the slips to move wider, and as a collective of catchers behind the wicket, you can cover more ground. This is possible, and the higher level of cricket you play, it is something to consider. However, there is certainly an inherent danger in going too wide, as it will affect your keeping in two ways:

• It makes it much harder to take leg-side deliveries because you have further to travel

• Often, outside-edge chances are missed because your

initial movement direction sends your body weight down the leg side, and when the outside edge comes, you do not have time to adjust and go in the opposite direction.

A crucial element of standing back to seam bowling is not getting wrong-footed.
JACK RUSSELL

The majority of missed outside-edge chances are because the keeper was standing too wide, and their weight initially transferred towards the leg side, thus making it difficult to adjust their body position in time to move back in the opposite direction. To explain this further we will use the example of an outswing bowler who starts the ball on a line towards leg stump. If you are standing wider than an off-stump line, your instincts will tell you to start moving towards the leg side, because if the ball does not swing, it will miss leg stump and continue in its original direction. However, if the ball does swing, and the batter gets an outside edge, your weight may be planted on your left leg, or even worse, your left leg will be in the air! It will then need to plant again, enabling a firm base to be established prior to pushing off to effect the catch away to your right.

Ultimately, as long as you have a clear view of the bowler's release, then you do not need to go any wider.

An important element of standing back to seam bowling is positioning. Be careful not to set your stance too wide of the off stump. Ideally you never want to be taking the ball with your weight committed to the leg side, in case the batsman edges the ball, as this makes the catch more difficult. Other things to consider are not getting set too early, keeping your posture throughout the catch and mentally being ready to move as the ball arrives at the batsman.

PETER MOORES

In fact, if it is an inswing bowler, bowling over the wicket and wide of the crease, you could consider starting even straighter with your left foot on middle stump. From this angle, even if balls are left outside off stump, by the time they reach you they will be in line with the stumps or maybe even beyond leg stump.

So, to summarise, your stood-back distance should be determined by the pace and bounce in the wicket, with your left foot initially aligned with off stump, although this can be repositioned depending on the type of bowling and your experience of it.

There are times when you will need to stand wider than off stump, for a left-arm over-the-wicket bowler, and even further for a right-arm bowler, bowling round the wicket. To judge the starting point, your main consideration is to ensure you have a clear view as the bowler releases the ball. As long as you can see the bowler's release, you are wide enough. If the bowler is predominantly swinging the ball away from a right-handed batter, then you may want to stand wider still.

When Stuart Broad comes round the wicket to left-handed batsmen my starting point will vary depending on how much the ball is moving, but a general starting point is my right foot on middle and off, which gives me a clear sight of release, but I can also get down the leg side. If it is a quick pitch, then I start wider. It is good to have a starting point close to the stumps as this is a better angle for judging lbw and going with outside edges.
TOM MOORES

Set-up, pre-delivery, balance, ready position

Once you have judged where you need to stand, at the bowler's release position you also need to remember that this is your finishing point, and that any pre-delivery movement needs to end at that exact point. That is why many wicketkeepers mark this point, so they know where they need to trigger to. Some also make a starting mark for their trigger.

As discussed in the previous chapter, as the bowler releases the ball, you want to establish a strong base, and a 'ready' position that you can move quickly from if needed. This ready position can be adjusted slightly depending on the bounce in the wicket. If the ball is arriving consistently low and reaching you at knee height, then you can bend your knees more to help you get lower, as the majority of balls and dismissal chances will come at that height. Similarly, on bouncier pitches you can set yourself higher. However, you will still need a flex in the knee to give you the base and spring to move quickly should the need arise.

Diving is discussed later in this chapter, but if there is a need to dive, ideally you want to be travelling in a straight line towards the ball. How you present your set-up will enable you to do this.

If you are too high, you will go up and over the ball; too low, and it will be above your head.

Importantly, remember to have an even spread of weight across both legs, as this will ensure that you are well balanced. It also ensures a full range of movement to either side, forward or back. Remember the point earlier about planting too much weight in one direction, as this will have an adverse effect on your ability to take a chance in the opposite direction.

Where to take the ball

If you are standing correctly and it is a consistent bowler, your bread-and-butter take will be coming straight at you, and on a reasonable wicket, somewhere around waist height. There are two main methods here:

- Step to the side of the ball and create a giving area to the side of your body
- Stay in line and take the ball into your body

Each method is acceptable. Try them both and decide which works best for you. We will give you the benefits of each.

When stepping to the side and creating a giving area to the left of your body, it is important to get the timing right. Usually, the hands are extended in front of the body, and the process of catching the ball starts here. As the ball is about to enter the gloves, the wicketkeeper should chassé to the right and take the ball on the left side of the body.

It is important that the catch is initiated in front of your body, ensuring that you do not move too early, as this enables your head to stay in line with the ball as long as possible. It also means that if the ball starts to swing towards the leg side, you can adjust to take it. As you chassé and bring the ball into your side, it enables your head to move and your eyes to track the ball all the way into the gloves until the catch is fully complete.

A lot of wicketkeepers like this method because of the increased giving area it creates, which can be very important when keeping to quick bowling. Another reason is that it gets the wicketkeeper's feet moving for each delivery, which can help if the ball is edged. It also shows energy to the team and, as discussed later, a wicketkeeper has an important role to play in energising the team.

However, this method does not enable you to cover more ground. That is a myth, because the taking of the ball always starts in line with the body and head, and most keepers resort to staying in line with the ball with their body behind it if a faint edge is produced off the bat.

Watch Jos Buttler or Tim Paine to see a good example of this method.

For those who prefer to take into the body, again your hands will have to start slightly in front of you, but this time there will be a reduced giving area as you take the ball into your body. However, a massive giving area is not always necessary and it only needs to be enough to complete the take effectively and safely. There is potential for overdoing the giving of the ball, and that is evident when your hands stop tracking the line of the ball. If it is not taken cleanly, and you have a very flamboyant give, the ball can come out of the gloves.

Some wicketkeepers prefer taking the ball into their bodies as this ensures that their head is always in line with the ball throughout the catching process. However, it is not as easy to follow the ball to the final moment the catch is completed. Primarily it is a simpler method, as there are fewer moving parts, hence less chance of error. Similar to a batter who does not have a big trigger, with this take the whole process of catching the ball is more straightforward.

Ultimately, your job is to catch the ball on a consistent and safe basis, so whichever method you go for you should have those points foremost in your mind.

Moving from side to side

The most important aspect of wicketkeeping stood back to the wicket is footwork. If you move your feet, half the job is done, and it helps with getting in line with the ball.

BEN DUCKETT
Nottinghamshire & England

There will, of course, be lots of deliveries that do not come straight at you, so you will need to move to one side or the other. Over the course of an innings, you will end up using a combination of two movements:

- A chassé (sometimes known as crabbing)
- Turning and running

We will assume a ball is moving away from the right-handed batter. Your initial movement will be with your right leg moving towards the line of the ball, and if you need to go further, your left foot then moves towards and next to your right foot (often connecting with it), the process continuing with your right foot moving away again. Once completed, you should be in a similar ready position to when you started:

This will ensure that as you begin the process of catching the ball, you are once again balanced with a solid base and your head is still.

Note for coaches

It is vital that as the wicketkeeper moves towards the ball, their head movement is minimal. This is similar to a batter coming down the wicket to the bowler. You would not coach a batter to have their head bobbing up and down as they come down the wicket. You would instruct them to keep their head as still as possible, even though their feet and body are moving. The same principle applies to a wicketkeeper's movement. Ensuring that the head remains as still and level as possible will enable the wicketkeeper to track the ball effectively, observe an edge clearly, react and respond quickly, and ultimately catch the ball.

In general, there are three moments when you need a clear view of the ball and to have your head as still as possible:

- As the bowler delivers the ball
- As the batter plays a shot (in case of an edged chance)
- As you take the ball (to help you take it cleanly)

The time when you turn and run will most likely be on a fast bouncy wicket where you are standing a long way back and have the time to do so. If you are close to the wicket you will either chassé or dive. A keeper should be encouraged to keep running to a minimum, the preference being to chassé, with the head, chest and feet facing the ball. This ensures that the hands and body are not cut off when taking the ball.

If running is necessary, aim for the feeling of the head being still, facing the ball and not bobbing up and down, endeavouring to keep your eyes as level as possible.

Drills for working both methods can be found in Chapter 9.

*Some wicketkeepers cross their feet behind each other when executing a chassé. South Africa's Quinton de Kock is one who sometimes does this. We do not recommend it, as whilst your feet are crossed, your balance/base is compromised, temporarily creating a position from which you cannot move.

Diving

Work on diving and one-handed catching – try to make your weaker hand as good as your strong hand so that it feels just as natural. Natural one-handed catching will get you out of trouble if you react late. If first slip is there, think low and forward. This will help train you to leave the higher, more comfortable catches for him.

ALAN KNOTT

At some point, moving your feet to get to the ball will not be enough and you will need to dive. This will often be through attempting to take a wide catch off an outside or inside edge. As this is a crucial moment in the game, you need to have regularly practised diving, even though diving for the ball usually happens infrequently during an innings.

The timing of the dive is purely instinctive, although you should be visualising and be mentally ready for the batter to edge the ball. Your reaction to the line of the ball informs you that you are unable to catch it unless you execute a diving movement response. The most important consideration when diving is getting your head going towards the ball, with your catching hand(s) leading the way. The fastest route is a straight line.

Again, your initial set-up is crucial. A strong balanced base coupled with a still head produces a great starting point from which to move. As the batter edges the ball, you can determine early in the ball's flight how much the deviation is. Then, having formed a strong base, you have the power in your legs to dive a considerable distance.

The difference between catching a ball when diving and taking a straight ball is that your elbows may not be bent; they will more likely be straight to give you maximum distance. Even though you are flying through the air, you still want that feeling of being relaxed, not tensed up. This time you take the ball laterally in line with your head and your give takes place behind this point, following the line of the ball. Once again, it is important not to have an excessive give, particularly with a one-handed catch, as in this instance it is good to feel the ball buried in the glove. Normally, one-handed catches sound a little louder than two-handed catches because of this. As with batting, look to have that feeling that you have time, you are letting the ball come to you, not being impatient, culminating in you going at it too early.*

It is really important that you have the sense that your hand(s) is on the line of the ball, waiting for it. If you have let your hands lead your head towards the ball you will achieve this. If you begin a dive with elbows bent, you will end up flicking them out just before you attempt to take the ball; getting the correct timing of this is very difficult because your hand moves in one direction, with the ball travelling in another.

Note for coaches

To compare with batting again, this would be like trying to drive a ball through square leg – the bat will be coming across the line and the timing of the bat downswing would have to be perfect to enable connection. The more you can achieve the feeling that a wicketkeeper's hand(s) is on a line of the ball waiting for it to arrive, the more success they will have with their diving catches.

Essentially, all coaches advocate catching with two hands where possible, and like knowing when to dive, your instincts will take over and tell you when you need to go with one hand. If you practise both catching methods regularly and have a routine that contains balls coming straight towards you, some where you have to move your feet, some where you have to dive two-handed, and some where you need to dive one-handed, both left and right, you will hone that instinctiveness for match situations. Thorough practice will ensure you have a good technique and enough confidence in yourself to take all these diving chances regularly.

*There is a school of thought that, when executing the diving process, if you dive towards the ball, as well as across, you can cut down the angle and catch a ball that otherwise would have been too far away if you had let it come laterally in line with your head. However, we have yet to see a wicketkeeper put this into practice at any level on a regular basis. It is really difficult to have your body weight going towards the ball and then have your hands give at the right moment to cushion the catch.

How should I land?

Previously, we have established that you need to go in a straight line with hand(s) extended, leading the head towards the ball. This will assist you in taking the ball cleanly. However, you still need to land without the ball coming out of the glove to achieve the catch and dismissal if the ball has been edged. We will look at two-handed diving first:

1. Take, give and roll to land on your left shoulder
2. Take, give and leave your arms extended
3. Take, give and bring your hands up into your body to land

The three methods are pictured here:

The first method allows a natural giving area. For a right-handed catch, as you take the ball you give behind you, and as you do so, you tuck your left shoulder underneath you. As you land, you take the force on your left arm and shoulder and then keep rolling. The opposite sequence applies for a left-handed catch. Often, wicketkeepers then bounce up from this dive.

This is a good method when the ball is knee height or above, as you have time before you hit the ground to effect the roll and land safely on the left side of your body. When the ball is knee height or lower there is not always time to effect the roll. This method also means that your hands do not touch the ground at any point, therefore the ball is less likely to bounce out should you not take it cleanly.

The timing of the roll is very important. Do not roll before you have caught the ball. It must be taken first. Both Jos Buttler and Jonny Bairstow favour this method and there is some good footage on YouTube of both of them.

The second method is great for catching balls that are lower than knee height and when you are at full stretch. There is not enough time to roll, and trying to do so may impede the catch, which is the most important thing.

Upon landing, try to keep your gloves off the floor, landing/ sliding on your arms, chest and thighs. It is really important to try not to let your gloves hit the ground too hard. It will be impossible for them not to, but the lesser the blow the better. This method allows for a great head position, watching the ball even as you land. This could be vital if you have not taken the ball cleanly, and it pops out slightly as you land. With your head facing the ball you may have the chance to react to this and adjust your hands accordingly.

The third method is commonly used by keepers who like to feel that security of the ball in the hands, allied with the body acting as an additional support to completing the catch. However, your hands will hit the ground hard, but the body can help keep the ball in if it was not taken cleanly. Additionally, if the ball was caught more in the fingers, a common occurrence when diving at full stretch, the ball simply will not stay in as you land, and may drop out with the actual movement of bringing the hands in. The Pakistan wicketkeeper, Sarfaraz Ahmed, tends to use this method.

The first method described is the preferred one as it creates a giving area, also ensuring your gloves never touch the ground. With continued practice, you will achieve the correct timing and consistency.

One-handed diving catches

Sometimes you just have to go with one hand. As discussed earlier, one-handed catching is an essential element of wicketkeeping. You may not do it often, but when you do it will be important, as it could be a match-defining moment, perhaps to dismiss the opposition's best player or to save five wides down the leg side in a tight limited-overs game. A brilliant one-handed catch can also give the team and the bowler a big lift. As a result of your catch, everyone else in the team ups their game. If you need to go one-handed for an edge, it is either because it is not carrying to slip (more on that later), or the batter is well set and there are no slips in.

The same three methods that applied for diving two-handed apply here:

1. Take, give and roll to land on your left shoulder
2. Take, give and leave your catching arm extended
3. Take, give and bring your hand up into your body to land

The first method has the benefits listed previously for a two-handed catch, but ultimately, if you are going with one hand, it is because it is absolutely necessary, and you are likely to be at full stretch. In that case it is very difficult to effect a roll. Also, unintentionally you can bring your hand off the line of the ball. If you put your catching arm out to the side of your body and then roll your left shoulder in, what happens to your catching arm? It comes in, and off the line of the ball. So, if you mistime the roll, you may end up not catching the ball, or possibly not diving as far as you need to.

The second method is recommended for the majority of one-handed diving catches. In terms of the catching hand staying on the line of the ball and leading your head to the ball, it helps achieve both. Movement of the hand after both the catch and the give are eliminated. With this method you should aim to take the ball laterally in line with your head and give behind, following the path of the ball. Your legs may even swing out towards the bowler as you land.

One of the differences between landing like this and when diving two-handed is that your non-catching arm is free, and if you leave this tucked into your body you can take the force of landing on your forearm, chest, stomach and thighs. If you achieve this landing, your catching hand will not hit the ground too hard, therefore increasing the likelihood that the ball will stay in the glove. With your head also in a great position throughout, it also enables you to watch the ball at all times and you can attempt any adjustments if you do not catch the ball cleanly, either in mid-air or upon landing.

Tim Paine and Brad Haddin are two good examples to watch some footage of for using this method.

For the third method you will need more time, so it will only really apply to catches at waist height and above, but it does enable you to bring your other hand to the ball and land as with a two-handed catch.

Ultimately, catching the ball is always the fundamental requirement, so whichever method you decide upon, if you practise it often enough you will have confidence to go for these difficult chances in games, and more often than not you will be successful.

Low diving takes

We greatly advocate letting the ball come to you when executing a diving catch, laterally in line with the head and then giving behind, following the line of the ball. However, there are times when you cannot wait and let the ball come to you, primarily if the ball is not going to carry to you. In this instance you need to take your hands forward towards the ball as you dive, and you literally 'scoop' the ball up from just above the ground.

In this instance, whether one- or two-handed, you will need to roll in the opposite direction to the first method above and roll on to your right shoulder.

Again, your hands should lead your head towards the ball, and the quicker you can assess the ball's landing position the better, and the quicker you can prepare to move forward to take the catch. As with any full-stretch dive, your arms will most likely be at full stretch, but if the ball is not going to carry, it means the pace has probably come off the ball, culminating in less 'give' being required when taking the catch. If your fingers are underneath the ball, touching the ground, you will be unable to give, so you simply need to ensure the correct timing of closing your hand(s) around the ball.

When should I not dive?

*If an edge is going to slip around shin high
or lower, you are entitled to go for it.*

JACK RUSSELL

A wicketkeeper should always adopt a positive mindset of going for chances, whether you can get two hands there or not. Mentally, you need to be prepared for a dismissal every ball, and if you are not mentally alert, you will not react and effect a wicket. We discuss mindset in greater depth in Chapter 6.

However, captains and bowlers are never happy if a wicketkeeper is diving in front of first slip trying to catch a ball one-handed – one that slip could have taken comfortably with two hands without moving.

So, should you go for it if first slip is in? The answer lies in the height that it would reach slip. Most slips prefer a catch at waist height and above. If the ball trajectory heads straight to them at a comfortable height, then you should allow those to be caught by the slip. You need to be mentally ready for the ones at knee height and below, as these are harder for slip to take and less likely to carry to them. It is the ones that are not carrying to slip that you must go for. If it is dropping short of slip, it is your catch, and you should attempt to go for it. Remember, first slip is always positioned further back than you are, so the ball may be even higher than waist high as it passes you. A clear understanding of the keeper and first slip relationship, in terms of positioning and catching ability, is essential.

Pitch gradients and cross falls may also determine your position in relation to the slips. Balls bowled uphill may come through slightly slower and higher, whereas balls bowled downhill may come through slightly faster and lower. Cross falls may mean that first slip is closer to you on an uphill gradient, or slightly further away from you on a downhill one.

Clearly, if there is no slip in place it is yours to try to catch! Go for it and try to pull off a stunner!

Diving summary

Diving is an essential element of wicketkeeping and needs a lot of practice to develop consistent technique, thus increasing the confidence to go for these catches in matches. Settle on a method that works for you. Finally, remember to be mentally prepared for each ball, as a chance could come, and you may need to dive to take it.

Note for coaches

Make sure your wicketkeeper practises their weaker side twice as often as their strong side. If right-handed, they will almost certainly find taking both one- and two-handed catches naturally easier on this side than to their left. They should aim at feeling as natural taking on their weaker side as they do on their favoured side, practising enough to eventually have two strong sides.

Stopping and taking balls that do not carry

Most pitches have some sort of variable bounce, and even if you have judged the correct place to set up, the ball will occasionally not carry. There is obviously no opportunity for a catch with these deliveries, so the important factor is taking it or stopping it to prevent any byes. There are two main methods to try:

Both of the photos above are good options, providing a good body area with which to stop the ball. The long barrier method provides the biggest area and allows for easy adjustment if the ball bounces erratically, as your head is closer to the ball and you can watch it all the way. However, if the ground in front of you is very worn, be careful that the ball does not leap up towards the head. If this is the case, then the pads together method is safer, and you have your pads to protect your legs. Do also consider wearing a helmet if the bounce is variable and the ground in front of you is very rough and produces unpredictable bounce.

If a ball is wide and does not carry, then it is easier to move across and execute a long barrier than to use the pads together method. Sometimes you will also need to dive and take/stop a ball that you know is not going to carry. Here it is as much about courage and keeping your eye on the ball as anything else.

The wobbling ball

Jimmy Pattinson wobbles the ball a lot after it beats the batsman, sometimes moving both ways up and down. It is important to stay relaxed in hands and body so you can adjust late. You will drop some wobbles and the whole team looks at you, but if you give away the odd bye it is not as important as dropping a catch. Focus on taking the nicks and make sure you take those, because the ball tends not to wobble when nicked.

TOM MOORES

Often, the ball will swing after it beats the batter. Usually, this is in the same direction it started to swing, but occasionally it swings in the opposite direction. Keepers can encounter a phenomenon where the ball keeps flipping in the air and can 'wobble', often moving slightly both ways, laterally and vertically. The wobbling ball is hard to take as you simply cannot be sure where it will end up when it reaches your catching zone. Balls not swinging or only swinging in one direction are easier to take as you can judge the end point accurately.

On TV, the wobbling ball is hard to pick up. Sometimes a thin edge creates a wobbling ball, and the commentators wonder why the catch was not taken, as it appeared to be a sitter. These are not sitters and it takes experience and the correct technique to judge them, particularly off the faster bowler. A ball coming at you at 85mph and constantly changing direction is very disconcerting.

So, if you have a bowler wobbling the ball, how should you take it? The most important element is to stay as relaxed as possible for as long as possible, to ensure your hands are relaxed as the ball reaches you. When it wobbles at you it is easy to tense up, but this inhibits movement of the hands and they are unlikely to adjust to any late movement.

There is also an option to stand closer. The theory is that you take the ball before it starts wobbling or has not wobbled for long, so changes in movement are decreased. This is true, and a viable method, but the drawback is you are now too close and have a reduced reaction time, thus making movements or diving for edges more difficult.

Another method is to come back with the ball as you take it. Liken this to stepping back to play off the back foot as a batter to a quicker bowler, thus giving yourself more time to play the ball. In this case catch the ball. As with any foot movement, you need that feeling of the head remaining still and level, enabling you to watch the ball closely, with your hands tracking the movement of the ball so you are able to make any necessary late adjustments.

If you are going to use this method when the ball is wobbling, then you will need to adjust your set-up point correctly so you are not too deep, thus ensuring that the ball still carries to you.

Note for coaches

How much a ball wobbles or not is also country dependent. It is very common in the UK but less so in other countries. This is due to different types of balls being used and the atmospheric conditions.

The flying saucer

Very occasionally, after pitching, the ball will end up with the seam horizontal rather than vertical and the ball can swing up or down (vertically) instead of side to side (laterally). Although rare, these are hard to take, but the key is to stay relaxed, not tense up and then move late to take the ball. Similar to playing the swinging delivery when batting, try not to move until you have the necessary information regarding where the ball will end up upon reaching you. The fortunate thing with a flying saucer delivery is that, although the ball swings up or down, it will only go in one direction and not both.

Reverse swing

Reverse swing can take place when an old ball suddenly starts to swing in the opposite way that you would expect it to normally. The theory is that the side of the ball that has been shined using sweat and saliva becomes heavier than the side that has not been shined. Normally, the shiny side would go through the air faster than the rough side, causing it to swing in the direction held by the rough side. With reverse swing this is reversed, as now the rough, non-shined side moves faster through the air than the wet heavy side. If a keeper is keeping to reverse swing, they may need to reposition their starting point as indicated earlier in this chapter. It is also important that you communicate with the bowler once the ball is reverse swinging so both of you know. The challenge is also to pick out which side the shiny side is in the bowler's hand, so you know which way they are trying to swing the ball.

Signals with the bowler

If a bowler has a good slower ball that they like to use on a regular basis, then it may be worth discussing with them having a signal system in place so that you are ready for it, especially if you cannot pick it in their hand. You are not allowed to run forward as the bowler runs in, but you can edge forward and be ready to move once they have let go.

Any signal needs to be subtle so that the batter does not pick up what is going on, so you might want to alter it between games or sessions.

In the photo, the bowler is shining the ball on his right thigh as he walks back to the mark. He would have discussed this with the wicketkeeper pre-match or spell. It does not matter what the signal is as long as you as wicketkeeper are looking out for it!

You will need to have a signal system between you and the bowler. To fool a batsman you could have several signals with only one being genuine.
ALAN KNOTT

Note for coaches

The modern-day wicketkeeper will find that they need to throw the ball for run outs a lot more than in years gone by. Particularly in T20 cricket and towards the end of any innings, batters may run a bye to the keeper in their quest for every possible run. It is essential, therefore, that the keeper practises their throws regularly, as run-out opportunities may be presented at both striker's and non-striker's ends. These throws could be from a standing, kneeling or sitting position. This is discussed in greater depth in Chapter 5, and practice drills can be found in Chapter 9.

Further, very often it is not possible to keep wicket to quick bowlers in the nets, because you would have to stand up to the wicket, due to the lack of space behind the stumps. To do so could be dangerous and very difficult, resulting in an injury or a drop in confidence. With this in mind, a good exercise is to stand behind, outside the nets, at the approximate distance you would in a match. You can then execute shadow takes, both off and leg side, getting a feel for the pace of the bowlers. This will be most beneficial for your home games, if you are regularly practising with mobile nets placed on your cricket square. Most first-class county grounds and many club grounds have mobile nets that have a full-width door at the back, so it can be opened to allow the keepers to keep realistically to the bowlers. This is great for slip fielders too, who can form a cordon with the keeper in practice.

THREE
STOOD UP TO SEAM BOWLING

I absolutely loved standing up to seamers. It was a great way to make it more fun and get you into the game with a chance of a leg-side stumping. You have to enjoy it and want to do it. Don't be afraid to make mistakes whilst being up to the stumps. Again, relax your hands and make them as wide as possible.

BEN DUCKETT

When stood up to seam bowling you need relaxed aggression. Aggression for speed everywhere in your body except below the elbows, where your lower arms and hands should be relaxed enough. If your thumbs are relaxed, lower arms and hands will be.

JACK RUSSELL

Should I stand up?

Standing up to Steve Mullaney in white-ball cricket is massive as you are able to keep the batter in his crease. He has to hit you from the crease, which is tougher the slower the bowler. It can keep the batsman deep in the crease, allowing the bowler to bowl fuller and the captain to set the field straight because they won't get the short ball to hit square. In red-ball cricket, where there is more movement, fewer slower balls and more chance of an outside edge, I would probably stand back to the same bowler.

TOM MOORES

Frequently, you will need to stand up to seam bowling, but the question you need to answer is: when is it right to do this? Just because you have the skills and confidence to do so does not mean you should. You need to evaluate whether there is a tactical advantage to you standing up to a seam bowler and whether this advantage outweighs standing back. If you stay back it increases the chances of you taking an edge should it be found, and it significantly increases the chances of you taking wide deliveries to the off or leg side, reducing the possibilities of giving away byes or additional wides.

The most common reasons for standing up to a seam bowler are:

- The batter is batting out of the crease or regularly moving out of the crease to play the ball, prompting you to remove that option, and adding the opportunity for a stumping. This will often be the case in a limited-overs match
- It is a low bouncing wicket, and the ball is not carrying consistently to you when stood back, meaning that outside edges may not carry. Standing up to the wicket will give you more chance of taking an edged catch
- The bowler is attacking the stumps, looking predominantly for bowled and lbw dismissals, so tactically you want to keep the batter stuck in the crease and playing off the back foot, to deliveries they should be going forward to
- A batter is well set and you, in discussion with the captain and bowler, want to try something different to break the batter's focus and rhythm, initiating a dismissal opportunity

If any of the above considerations outweigh the ones to stand back, then you should come up to the wicket. As with any skill it is important that you have practised it regularly, so you have the technique and confidence to do so. Another consideration is the bounce of the wicket. If the bounce is very inconsistent, then standing up to a seam bowler becomes very challenging and you may give away too many byes.

When deciding whether to stand up to a seam bowler, consider if there is outswing or out seam movement for outside edges and what genuine chance of a stumping there is. If the first outweighs the second, then you should stay back.

ALAN KNOTT

Where to stand

When you are either stood back to the seamers or stood up to the spin bowlers, your main consideration is whether you have a clear line of sight of the bowler at their point of release. As you are now stood up to a seam bowler, your second consideration is whether you are close enough to the stumps to effect a stumping.

A good starting point is having your left foot on the line of off stump, and as close to the bowling crease as you can without your gloves or any part of your body being in front of this line. If any of your body encroaches in front of the line as the bowler delivers the ball, it will be deemed a no ball, and you cannot effect a dismissal. Unless you have really small feet, a foot's length is a good guide to determine how far back from the bowling crease you set up, although you can stand back further as long as you can reach the stumps for a stumping opportunity.

Most current international wicketkeepers stand further than a foot's length back.

With your left foot on off stump, you should have a clear view past the batter to see the bowler releasing the ball, enabling you to pick up the line, length and any swing early in the ball's trajectory. If a bowler is bowling wide of the crease and swinging the ball in, you may want to adjust this starting point, with your left foot on middle or even leg stump. Similarly, if a left-arm-over bowler is bowling, you may have to go wider than off stump to see past the batter.* These are small adjustments, and you should still be close enough to effect a stumping if the chance presents itself.

THE PITCH

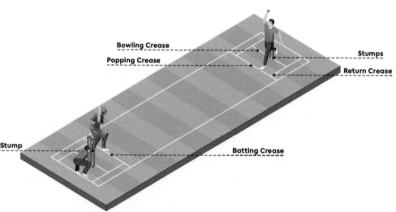

* A left-arm seamer swinging the ball back in to the right-hander can be challenging if you have set up wider to ensure a clear line of sight, as the swing can take the ball down the leg side. In this instance, think about widening your stance, so that your left foot can start more towards middle or leg stump, with your right foot

positioned well outside the off stump. This will keep your head outside off stump, ensuring a clear view of the bowler's release, but with your left foot closer to leg stump you are physically closer to getting down the leg side should you need to.

Stance and set-up

Don't worry about keeping your hands low to the ground until the ball pitches; there's no time for that and will make you slower. Gauge how soon they come up by the pace and bounce of the pitch.
JACK RUSSELL

It is still not essential to go down into a traditional stance. Assuming the bounce of the wicket is reasonably consistent, most balls will reach you at waist height if the bowler is regularly hitting a good length. Even on a low wicket, a good-length ball will reach you around knee height. A seam bowler will not normally get huge deviation from the pitch either, so there is less need to track the ball with your gloves from ground contact to glove contact. The only instance when you may set yourself very low is if the bounce is very inconsistent. It is easier to push up to take a high-bouncing delivery than it is to drop down to take a low-bouncing delivery. Additionally, if the bowler is trying to mainly bowl yorkers, the ball will come through to you predominantly at ankle height.

Any stance should be comfortable. Ensure a still head position and a strong balanced base, and this will enable you to move quickly should you need to, as there are times when you are stood up to seam bowling when you will need to move very quickly indeed. A good starting point to have your hands is around knee height as the bowler lets go of the ball, with your arms relaxed but not locked straight. There will not be too many deliveries where you have to take below here. Unlike keeping to spin bowlers, it is not necessary to have your gloves on the floor at this stage.

Note for coaches

If a player favours a wide stance, often suited to tall wicketkeepers, then with their left foot starting on off stump, they may find their head too far from off stump. In this instance, the left foot can start on middle or leg to gain the desirable head position.

Not many wicketkeepers do this, but there is no reason why you should not trigger into position stood up to a pace bowler, but the same principles apply – it must be consistently the same for each ball and you must have a solid base and still head on delivery. In this instance, you must also make sure your trigger is completed before you reach the bowling crease, thus negating a no ball being called.

Try to avoid bobbing your head and bouncing your gloves up and down as the bowler runs in. This can often lead to the head being on the move as the bowler lets go, therefore affecting how early you pick up the ball in its flight.

Essentially, stance is a personal preference. As long as you can see the ball and move quickly, that is ideal. If you prefer a traditional stance and it works for you, then use it. The one advantage of a traditional stance stood up to any type of bowler is that your feet are close together and it is easier to get your pads together as a second line of defence should you miss the ball with the gloves.

If you are someone who naturally has a very wide stance, your left foot should start on middle or leg stump. If you start on off stump, your head and hands will be too wide of the off stump. Similar to standing back, a lot of wicketkeepers mark the spot where they want to position their left foot.

In addition to being close enough to effect a stumping, there is another important reason not to stand further away from the bowling crease: if an edge is found, then the ball has less distance to travel and therefore deviate before you have to take it.

Occasionally you will have a batter in front of you who has a wide bat swing, perhaps starting the bat towards gully. This can often get in front of your eyes and inhibit you viewing the bowler as they run in. Most batters will adjust this as the bowler delivers, but if they do not, then you will have to move in some way. Remember that a clear sight of the bowler's release point is essential. This could be standing wider or starting higher. Hopefully, only a small adjustment is needed, and if you need to move, remember to have that feeling that the body is moving but the head is still. It is a controlled movement. If you have a clear view of the bowler releasing the ball, you should be able to adjust and take it, even if you have adjusted your set-up slightly.

Note for coaches

It is worth practising this when you are doing shadow batting drills with your wicketkeepers. Have your bat swing outwards to gully and get the bat in front of their eyes to see how they adjust. It is a skill that can be worked on and a game plan can be devised should this happen in a match.

Taking the ball

The catching area of the hands remains the same and you still only need to give as much as necessary. However, this may be increased if the bowling is quick. The less give you need, the quicker you will get the ball back to the stumps. But you have to *take the ball first* before you go for a stumping, so this is your main consideration on how much you give. You must also consider whether you bring your right foot back to allow your body to open, thus creating a giving area on the right-hand side of your body. This is inevitable if the ball bounces very high. With all takes, try to keep your head as close to the ball as possible.

If you have your left foot starting on off stump, then most good-length deliveries will be heading towards your right hip. You should try to have the feeling that your hands are on the line of the ball, or moving outwards to take it, rather than coming back in to take most balls. The reason for this is that if you are standing too wide and you have to come in towards the stumps to take balls outside the off stump, the hands are heading in the wrong direction should the batter edge the ball. It is very difficult for your hands to then change direction. You want to get the feeling that your hands are going with an outside edge to take the catches on a consistent basis.

If you can keep your hips parallel to the crease with a small give whilst taking the ball consistently, this is the ideal because it is quicker to get back to the stumps if there is a stumping opportunity. However, a lot of wicketkeepers do take their right leg back as they take the ball stood up to seam bowling, thus removing the parallel alignment. The two main reasons are to create a bigger giving area and to give you more time, like that of a batter moving back towards the stumps to play off the back foot. You are giving yourself time to take the ball. The movement does not have to be a massive one, and you should leave your left foot by the stumps so that you can get your body weight and the ball back if there is a stumping opportunity. This side-on photo shows this method in action:

As with any movement, this needs to be done with control and in a way that ensures the head has that feeling of stillness we talked about previously. Like taking the ball to the side of your body stood back, giving with the right leg allows a great head position to watch the ball all the way into the gloves. Jos Buttler, Jonny Bairstow, Tim Paine, MS Dhoni and Sarfaraz Ahmed all take their right leg back on taking the ball, so if this is your preferred method you will be in good company! This movement is often called the 'K' position.

Note for coaches

Start your practice without a batter or other coaching aids and simply focus on technique. Do not ask the wicketkeeper to go back to the stumps for a stumping at this stage. First, get them used to the rhythm of taking the ball cleanly on a consistent basis. Then you can progress by identifying some balls for a stumping attempt. Then introduce a shadow batter and see if the keeper can hold the technique with the batter there. You can then ask the batter to give the occasional stumping chance, looking to increase the speed of the stumping as you progress. Remember that the wicketkeeper *must take the ball first*.

To simulate edges, the best piece of equipment you can use is some foam pipe lagging, replacing the batter's bat. These can be obtained very cheaply from any hardware store. They offer a realistic amount of deflection more often than not, and they do not break! Drills to practise this take can be found in Chapter 9.

One major technical issue to watch out for when standing up to the quicker bowlers, and even spin bowlers, is the head flinching and moving away from the line of the ball. This can often happen as the batter plays a shot. It is almost an involuntary movement, where the mind is telling you to protect the head. The two major drawbacks here are that:

- Your head gets taken away from the line of the ball, and you stop looking at it.
- Your arms start to stiffen and tense up – often culminating in straight arms and tense elbows.

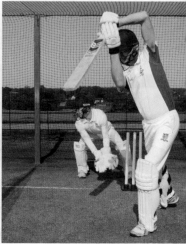

These two issues will hamper your ability to take the ball cleanly. The only way to stop this is to practise on a regular basis with a batter in front of you swinging the bat to simulate shots with a three-step progression:

1. Missing all of the time
2. Missing some of the time
3. Playing normally

Initially, do a lot of the first practice, then progress to two, and then to three. By this stage you are working your powers of concentration as much as technique. You must stay mentally alert to take every ball.

Taking the fuller deliveries

The fuller the ball, the harder it is to take, increasing the likelihood of your head flinching. It is a more difficult take because you must stay lower for longer, and there is less time to react to any late swing or seam movement. If the batter edges it, they are likely to be driving, therefore you have a swinging bat in front of your eyeline and there is further distance for the ball to travel to your gloves, compared to when the batter is defending or playing off the back foot. In theory, an edge from a cut shot should be the easiest nick for you to take as the ball has less time to deviate before it reaches your gloves, because the bat is nearer to them.

It is imperative for the fuller takes that you stay brave and keep the head looking at the ball for as long as possible, ideally seeing it pitch to judge any movement. Ironically, although the head tends to flinch more for the fuller deliveries, you are actually much less likely to get hit in the head from this length, although balls landing in bowlers' footmarks can occasionally cause the ball to react unpredictably.

Even if you do not do it regularly, you may find giving with the right leg very beneficial now to give yourself that extra bit of time to complete the take. Do remember, however, that if a batter is playing an attacking shot, this increases the chances of a dismissal opportunity with them either edging the ball or overbalancing and dragging their foot out of the crease for a stumping chance.

A yorker-length delivery may only come through at ankle height. Again, head position is vital. Stay brave and low and it is essential to have your elbows straight so that your gloves get low to the ground. Try to keep your elbows relaxed though, so there is still some give as the ball hits the gloves. It is also advantageous to bring your legs together so there is a second line of defence with your pads should you miss the ball with your gloves.

If the ball is wide, try to line up your right leg with the ball as a second line of defence. You can still come back with the right leg as well if this is your preferred method. However, do keep your left leg close to the stumps, unless body momentum does not allow you to do so. This will allow you to still be able to get to the stumps if required.

Note for coaches

A good practice for this length delivery is to have a chair in front of the wicketkeeper and the ball delivered underneath it, replicating the ball going underneath the batter's bat.

Leg-side takes

The biggest difficulty with leg-side takes is the fact that the batter obscures your view of the ball as it passes them. Momentarily, the ball is totally lost from view. The length of time slightly varies, depending on whether the batter is playing a front- or back-foot shot. The ball is hidden slightly longer on a front-foot shot, as the batter's body profile is longer than on a back-foot shot. You do not have much time, unless the ball is really wide, between realising the ball is going or could go down the leg side to actually having to move to it. Ideally, your head, hands and feet would all move together but this is rarely possible to do. Because the catching of the ball is the main priority, it is your hands that will have to go first, with your head and feet following.

Your aim is to still see the ball pitch, but this is not as important stood up to a seamer as it is to a spinner. However, you should try to keep your head off side for as long as possible, enabling you to see the ball pitch. If you move too early to the leg side, the ball is lost behind the batter's body profile for longer, thus making a clean take more difficult.

It is imperative that you try to catch the ball in the ideal area discussed in Chapter 1, as this will help to make sure that your hands go far enough across, ensuring that the ball is in the hands, not just on to the fingers.

Note for coaches

See the drill in Chapter 9 where the wicketkeeper takes the ball one-handed only in the opposite hand to the side that the ball is being taken. This is really good practice to get the hands in the correct position for leg-side takes and can be done with a simple underarm feed. It is also good practice for coming back to the stumps for one-handed stumpings.

After your hands have gone towards the line of the ball, your left foot and head should follow. Your right foot should then chassé across to plant itself behind the stumps (this is important for getting back to the stumps for a stumping chance). Your left foot then establishes a strong base. If you have planted your right foot by the stumps and have established a good base on your left foot, you can push off this foot to effect the stumping, helped by moving your body weight back to the stumps. Once you are highly competent, the hands can start moving back towards the stumps as your body moves in the opposition direction.

If you have had to go a long way to get the ball, it may be quicker to get back to the stumps with one hand. If you have caught the ball in the sweet spot, it should be easy to get the ball firmly gripped to get back to the stumps quickly. If it is not such a clean take, make sure you adjust to get the ball firmly gripped before going back to the stumps. If you rush it, the ball may fall out before you get back.

Some wicketkeepers find it advantageous to step back slightly with their left leg as they move across, thus creating a giving area again, in addition to allowing themselves more time to see the ball.

Sometimes the ball is so wide on the off or leg side that you simply are not going to get to it with footwork, so you will need to dive. But if you have a good strong base in your stance, you should have a good platform to push off from. All other diving principles apply, and when you are practising, why not see if you can also flick the ball back for a stumping, even though you are a long way from the stumps.

Similar to diving, practise leg-side takes to both left- and right-handers, and whichever is your least natural side, practise that side twice as often as the other.

Should I always take the bails off after every delivery?

Whether you should take the bails off after taking the ball is personal preference. It certainly lets the batter know how sharp you are and some captains and coaches you play for like this too. It is definitely beneficial if the batter plays an attacking shot, as this is when there is more chance of them overbalancing and dragging their foot out of the crease. Any batter who does not establish a strong front-foot base for any shot becomes a potential stumping victim. It is also beneficial if it keeps you mentally sharp, active and buzzing. This is good for you and good for the team and the effect it can have on them.

The most important thing, though, is to make sure you *take the ball first*. If the ball does take the outside edge and you have started to move towards the stumps too early, it will hamper your chance of completing the catch. 'Aggression with relaxed hands' is a good phrase to remember when standing up. Quick hand speed is essential for completing a stumping. Do not give too much as you take the ball, as any split second saved can mean the difference between the attempt being given out or not out. Many young players will try to smash all three stumps down when attempting a stumping, which invariably means they take a big wind-up to gain hand speed. This will lead to the attempt taking longer, therefore the batter may then be given not out. There should be no backswing, and one bail removed is all that is required to identify a top-quality keeper.

FOUR

STOOD UP TO SPIN BOWLING

Keeping your hands down so they come up with the bounce of the ball will
help you find rhythm. Mentally, you need to be able to focus on the bowler
and the ball and take the batter out of the equation. Stay relaxed and
try and get your head in line with the ball wherever possible.

PETER MOORES

Standing up to spin bowling is described by purists as the true art
of wicketkeeping, and certainly when keeping to a good spinner
you are always in the game and you can effect a lot of dismissals.
Numerous methods and considerations apply to spin as they do
to seam, so we have tried not to repeat too much in this chapter.

*Keeping to orthodox spin is more difficult than keeping to wrist
spin, especially at the higher standard of cricket you play. The
length they bowl is fuller and has less bounce from the pitch and
far fewer deliveries beat the bat. A keeper's concentration skills are
tested to the full. Although keeping to wrist spin might be easier, it
is only easier if you can pick every delivery.*

ALAN KNOTT

Where to stand

A clear line of sight of the bowler delivering the ball is once again
your prime consideration. One of the most important factors of

wicketkeeping to spin bowling is that you can read (pick) the delivery that the bowler is bowling (more on this later). Leg-spinners usually have the most variations, but orthodox spinners can also vary how much they turn each delivery or bowl arm balls. All spinners will vary the pace they bowl at and, of course, an orthodox off-spinner may be able to bowl a doosra.

For these reasons it is important that the keeper can see past the batter to the bowler's hand as the run-up commences, to detect any changes of grip, continuing to see the hand as the ball is released. Positioning your left foot on off stump is a good starting point, dependent upon how wide your natural base is, as discussed in the previous chapter.

In terms of distance back from the stumps, one foot's length back is again a good measure, but as long as you can reach the stumps, further back is fine. You should find that you can keep helmet and hands behind the bowling crease but be close enough to effect a stumping. Mark the spot if it helps or draw a line back from off stump.

Another consideration concerning where you stand is how much turn there is in the wicket. If it is a high-turning wicket, keeping to an off-spinner, you may want your left foot further into the stumps. Conversely, you could stand slightly wider if it is a leg-spinner bowling. You could also widen your stance. As long as you can still see the bowler releasing the ball, any adjustments are acceptable. Additionally, the same considerations regarding set-up position apply to keeping to spinners as they do to seamers, whether it is a right-arm round-the-wicket bowler or a left-arm over-the-wicket bowler.

Stance and set-up

The most important aspect of standing up to spin bowlers is to stay down and come up with the bounce of the ball.
DAVID RIPLEY

To aid with tracking the ball with your gloves, one of the most important factors of wicketkeeping to spin bowling, particularly orthodox spin bowling because it is usually a fuller length, is that you stay down with gloves on the ground or as close to that as possible. You should then come up with the bounce of the ball, tracking it with your gloves all the way into them. Most opportunities are missed when a wicketkeeper comes up too early and the ball hits the fingers, rather than going deep into the hands, encouraged by sustaining a low hands and body position.

It is therefore necessary to set yourself lower for spin bowling than you would when stood up to seam bowling, ensuring that your gloves can be low to the ground, if not touching it. Many wicketkeepers therefore adopt a more traditional stance as this makes it easier to keep their gloves on the ground. It is also possible to achieve this with a wider stance and simply bend your knees more. Both set-ups are pictured here:

As when batting, you have more time when keeping to spin. A batter may not trigger at all to a spin bowler, or certainly a lot less than they would to a fast bowler. There are few wicketkeepers that initiate a trigger movement when stood up to a spin bowler.

Although you may need to move quickly at some stage, you want your body to be as relaxed as it can be, so you are less likely to tense up, thus inhibiting movement.

If you feel that your weight is going forward towards the ball, it is worth noting that many wicketkeepers feel that it is an advantage to have their weight more on their heels than on the balls of their feet in their set-up. This is not possible with a traditional stance. It is easier to keep balance this way. Similarly, if a batter is regularly falling over to the off side in their set-up, coaches will ask them to keep their weight on the heels and remain flat-footed.

Note for coaches

Watch out for excessive head movement in the pre-delivery stance. Some movement is tolerable, but the ideal is to have the head completely still as the bowler releases the ball, ensuring the ball is picked up as early as possible in its flight and that any variations can be spotted immediately. To train a wicketkeeper to keep their gloves on the floor as the ball pitches, a suitable drill is to execute some overarm bounce throws to them, occasionally not releasing the ball. You can then determine whether they remained still, with gloves still on the floor at the point of release. Can they also replicate that with a batter there?

Taking the ball

I found allowing my legs to straighten a little while keeping the hands down worked for me when I was stood up to the wicket.
PETER MOORES

We have now determined the need to stay low and track the ball, and it is still important to keep your hands and arms relaxed. However, if you stay in your stance you will find it difficult to come up with the bounce of the ball and your knees can get in the way, so you need to start straightening your legs but leaving your hands and head low, just before the ball hits the ground, so that you can come up with the bounce of the ball.

Similar to standing up to seam bowling, it is preferable to stay chest on and take the ball into your body or slightly to the right-hand side. You do not need as much give as you do when stood up to seam bowling, and there are usually more stumping opportunities to spin bowling than seam, so remaining chest on ensures a quicker route back to the stumps.

When the ball really bounces you will see some wicketkeepers rotate their hips, with or without moving their left foot back, so that their chest does not restrict the catching area. Others move their head and upper body inside the line of the ball and lift their right leg to balance out.

Similar to standing up to seam bowling, many wicketkeepers like to give themselves time and move back slightly with their right leg to take the ball.

There is no right or wrong in all three methods, it is your personal preference. The first two allow quicker stumpings than the one taking your right leg back but remember you cannot complete a stumping unless you *take the ball first*, so that is your overriding consideration when deciding which method works best for you.

Note for coaches

Why not have your wicketkeeper try all three methods ten times and see which is the most consistent. If you stand square on, you could even time how long it takes to effect a stumping from taking the ball to taking the bails off.

An instinctive head flinch can also be a problem for wicketkeepers stood up to spin bowling, so practise regularly with a batter swinging a bat, stump or pipe lagging in front of you and remember the shadow batting sequence:

1. Missing all of the time
2. Missing some of the time
3. Playing normally

Initially, do a lot of the first drill, then progress to two and then to three. By this stage you are working your powers of concentration as much as technique. You have to stay mentally ready to take every ball.

Picking the spin bowler's delivery

One of the most important aspects of standing up to spin bowlers is watching their hand closely to pick which way the ball is turning.
BEN DUCKETT

It is a great advantage if you can pick the delivery from the bowler's hand rather than having to read it off the pitch. You will know before landing which way it is likely to go and you can mentally prepare for that outcome, as well as get yourself physically ready to adjust with the ball. Leg-spinners tend to have the most variations, but there are several for the orthodox spinner as well. Below are some pictures of hand positions for various deliveries that you may encounter. These will give you an idea of what to look out for with the spin bowlers you have to keep to.

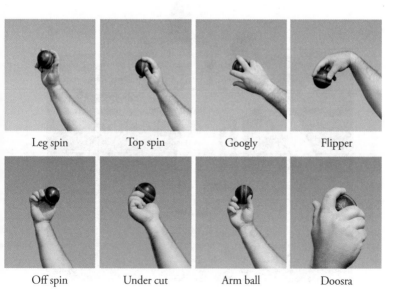

| Leg spin | Top spin | Googly | Flipper |

| Off spin | Under cut | Arm ball | Doosra |

Leg-side takes

As with standing up to seam bowling, the biggest difficulty with leg-side takes is that the batter obscures your view of the ball as it passes them. The method for going leg side can alter for spin bowlers as usually you will have more time due to the slower bowling speed. Whether you move early or late depends on the line and length of the delivery, but to gauge effectively how much turn and bounce there is, you must see the ball pitch.

In the picture above, the ball is of a good length from an off-spinner pitching in line with leg stump. However, the wicketkeeper has not committed early and has kept his head off side to see the ball land. Once he has seen this, he then has a good idea where it will end up once it has passed the batsman.

A common fault is that a wicketkeeper will go too early and get their head behind the batter as the ball lands. Unable to see the ball pitch, it is guesswork as to how much it has turned and bounced, so their gloves may end up in the wrong position. The keeper should try to stay off side as long as possible, enabling them to see the ball pitch. If they move too early to the leg side, the ball is lost behind the batter's body profile for longer, thus making a clean take more difficult. This is the main reason why a keeper does not take the ball down the leg side. Another is bringing the hands up when moving across. This will be discussed later.

In the picture above, what do you notice about the wicketkeeper's left foot? Here it has started to move leg side even though his head and body weight are still to the off side. That is the subtle difference when keeping to spin: you have time to move your feet first, so it is not the hands that go first as with keeping to seamers.

You will start to move your feet but leave your head in a position to see the ball pitch. Then push off your right leg to transfer your weight on to your left leg, then the head and hands follow. Having seen the ball pitch, you should have a good idea of where it will be upon reaching the gloves. Again, a chassé is the preferred method, remembering to leave your right foot planted by the stumps so you can get back to the stumps for a stumping.

Moving across parallel, lifting your left leg, or taking it back, are all viable methods. Use whichever works best for you. If you are struggling to take the ball consistently, you may consider taking the left leg back to give you more time.

You will lose track of the ball during this take but try not to tense up as you lose sight of it and keep relaxed so you give with the ball upon it reaching your gloves.

Note for coaches

If you do not have a shadow batter, why not use some tall cones or a box/chair, vertical kit bag, football player mannequin etc? Any object that can get in the wicketkeeper's eyeline, obscure their view, thus simulating a batter. Once your wicketkeeper is very consistent, why not start timing how quickly the bails can be removed, and if you have a shadow batter, initiate some routines where the batter attempts to hit the ball leg side and overbalances, lifting the back leg. See if your keeper can beat the batter back.

When the ball is fuller or much wider, you will need to move leg side before the ball pitches in order to see it pitch, as in the sequence opposite.

Here the wicketkeeper has moved his hands across, along with his left leg, and can view the ball pitch from a position down the leg side. Notice also how low his gloves have remained throughout. It is very common for a wicketkeeper to straighten their knees whilst moving leg side but it is still important to keep those hands low and come up with the bounce of the ball. It is so difficult to get back down again if the ball keeps low.

It is sometimes more challenging to take leg-side deliveries from leg-spinners because they are often targeting pitching on leg to turn to off. If they miss this line and go further outside leg stump and the ball does not turn, it will miss the batter's pads and you need to take it. However, the difficulty is that, due to the line, you may not see the ball pitch if the batter is on the front foot and gets their legs between the line of the ball and your head.

If it were an off-spinner, you would move leg side early to see it pitch leg side, safe in the knowledge that the ball will continue heading in that direction. However, with a leg-spinner it can turn back towards the off side, so it is not as easy to commit early. If you know the bowler, you may be able to gauge whether the ball is likely to turn back to the off side or skid on down the leg side. This can often be judged on pace. The quicker the ball, the more likely it is to skid on; the slower the ball, the more likely it is to turn.

It is really important when you move leg side for any take that you do not lift your gloves – they should remain low to the ground, still tracking the bounce of the ball and coming up with it. If you have kept your legs bent as you chassé, this should keep your gloves low to the ground. Imagine your arms are just hanging as you move across and keep them loose and relaxed.

Note for coaches

For speed and to check that the ball is still going into the sweet spot of the gloves, ask your wicketkeeper to take the bails off one-handed after they have caught the ball down the leg side. If they have caught the ball correctly, they should be able to secure the ball in their right hand and get this back to the stumps. It is worth timing them to see whether they are quicker with one hand or two. If they are much quicker with one, then they could use this option for leg-side stumpings, even if they could use two hands.

Left-arm-over bowler targeting the rough

One of the toughest challenges a wicketkeeper will have to face is to keep to a spin bowler who is targeting the rough, usually outside the leg stump of a right-handed batter. Even more so if there is little turn in the 'good' part of the pitch. If the ball hits the good part, it can skid on in a straight line. If it hits the rough it can turn and bounce viciously, making a clean take even more challenging.

The type of bowler who most often attempts this strategy is a left-arm orthodox spinner bowling over the wicket to a right-handed batter, but it could also be a leg-spinner bowling round the wicket.

To attempt to judge these deliveries it is even more important to see the ball pitch. Depending upon how wide the rough is, you can set up outside leg stump:

The ball that hits the good part of the pitch continues on in a straight line to the wicketkeeper. The one that hits the rough ground turns towards or past the stumps. This now becomes your leg side. It should be noted that not many wicketkeepers use this method, but if you are giving a lot of byes away down the leg side by normally setting up on the off side, it is worth considering. Our advice is to try both leg-side and off-side set-ups and see which method allows you to take the ball consistently.

If you opt for an off-side set-up, remember you do not start taking your body weight leg side before the ball lands, as if it pitches and turns, the ball will head towards the off side and you will find it difficult to stop and adjust to go back in the other direction. Most catches will still come from an outside edge to this type of bowling, or similarly a stumping past the outside edge.

Not many wicketkeepers opt for a leg-side set-up for this type of bowling but do not be afraid of doing something different. Just think about how many different types of shots modern batters are playing each innings, which are now simply the norm. If it works for you it is the correct method to use.

Note for coaches

You can practise this in a turf net by roughing up part of the surface or practising at the other end, where the bowlers have been landing. If it is a true surface throughout, either on artificial or turf nets, you can put some debris down, such as mats, cones, clothing, screwed- up paper, etc., to simulate the challenges encountered when keeping on these particular types of ground conditions.

*With all spinners, spend as much time taking
deliveries from them in practice as you can.*
JACK RUSSELL

Batters playing ramps and reverse sweeps

*The key aspect when a batsman goes for the ramp shot is
not to panic. You can give yourself room and back off.
I tend to jump up and back and make my hands big.
There's a 1 in 1,000 chance it may go in the glove.
I've got to time it right, just in case the batsman misses it.*
TOM MOORES

When batters are playing these shots there are some options you can try to prevent the shot going for runs. It is important that you hold your position for as long as possible as they may of course miss the shot, and there may still be a stumping chance. With a reverse you can be ready to dive to your right to stop/ take a catch, and a wicketkeeper like MS Dhoni even sticks out his right leg to try to stop the ball.

*With the reverse sweep, I try and stick out a leg and I always
believe it is important to have a mindset to try and influence the
game. You've still got to hold the line and expect them to miss it –
just like any other shot. When a batsman paddle sweeps, you can
move leg side early and try and take a catch. Sarah Taylor took a
brilliant one for England doing this where the batter lofted the ball
slightly and she dived and took the catch.*
TOM MOORES

With a ramp shot there is less chance of a stumping, so as the batter sets up for this you can move backwards and towards the line they are shaping up to play. If they move in front of you, you will have to move your head and/or body to still view the ball. Ramps always go up off the bat, so if they do not connect sweetly there may be a chance of a skied catch. Remember, even if you start to move, keep watching the ball closely.

FIVE

OTHER DISMISSAL OPPORTUNITIES

I get a lot of run outs in T20 cricket. I will get one a game to roll at the stumps, last over of the innings. To ensure my fielding and throwing skills are sharp, I always join in the fielding drills with the other players. In the modern game it is important your fielding is sharp as you can still get in the team if your batting's good as a batsman. The current England Test team is a good example with often three wicketkeepers in the team together.

TOM MOORES

Catches from the edge of the bat will almost certainly make up most of the dismissal opportunities that come your way, as will stumpings if you have a good spinner in the team. There are also several other dismissals that you must prepare and practise for.

The skyer

When a batsman top edges a hook or pull shot, try and cover the ground as early as possible, so ideally you don't have to catch the ball on the move, and you can have a nice still base as you make the catch. Personally, I prefer a normal catching technique instead of reversing my hands. I try and create a bowl for the ball to go in.

TOM MOORES

A reasonably common dismissal for a wicketkeeper to take is the top edge from a pull, hook or sweep shot, occurring more often stood back than stood up. The key to taking any chance like this is to keep your eye on the ball at all times, and if it requires chasing behind the direction you were originally facing, try not to start spinning in several different directions. Try to do the hard work early and establish a solid base with a still head prior to catching the ball. When setting up the catch, all the energy is in the lower half of the body, i.e., the legs, and upon taking the catch you should have a relaxed top half, i.e., the hands.

Because of the height that the ball goes when these chances go up you have a lot of time to think about it, but if you think you can get there it should be your catch and no one else's, as you will have a better chance of taking it wearing gloves. Clear your mind of doubt, call for it and get moving. Keep your eye on the ball all the way if you can and take deep breaths. It is common when a catch goes up and you realise it is yours to catch that there will be some butterflies, so your breathing is important. As with any other aspect of wicketkeeping, if you have put enough practice in, you will be confident about going for the catch and completing it effectively.

Note for coaches

A good drill to replicate match conditions is for you to stand in the batting crease facing your wicketkeeper, who should be standing back from the wicket to replicate receiving from a fast bowler. From their ready position you hit the ball over their head and side to side to replicate a top-edged pull shot. Ensure that the wicketkeeper is back into their ready position between each attempt. A similar drill can be done for top-edged sweeps with the wicketkeeper stood up.

Run outs – direct hits

Although they do not count towards your personal tally, there are often run out chances that a wicketkeeper can effect during a match, particularly in a limited-overs match. These can be equally important to turn the course of a game and lift your team.

Most frequent is the one where the batter attempts to push and angle a single run into the off or on side when you are stood up to the wicket, although this can also happen when you are stood back if the ball is played behind square. If it is not hit with power you can sometimes get there in time to effect a run out, usually at the bowler's end because the striking batter is running from the crease, from a relatively stationary starting position. However, the opportunity could be at either end, and hopefully your team will be attuned to the opportunity as well and give you a sound call.

Apart from the throw itself, the most important feature here is to be mentally alert for these opportunities every time the batter looks for these shots. If you are not, you will react late. Anticipation is the key. Observe the batter's body shape and bat downswing speed. If you react well the first time this happens in a match, you may also stop some singles, with the batters reluctant to take an excessive risk. Therefore, you have saved some runs just by showing positive dynamic intent.

To throw effectively you will need to get the glove off your throwing hand. You may need to pull it off with the other hand or you may be able to force it off with a powerful swing of the arm. The main thing is for the glove to end up behind you so that you do not trip on it or it hits the ball. Pulling the glove off is usually the quicker option, as it provides better balance and allows a faster running technique.

Remember, if you throw your glove on the floor and subsequently a throw comes in and hits the glove, it is five runs to the opposition, similar to if the ball hits an unattended helmet stored on the ground behind the keeper. Therefore, it is advisable to throw the glove well away from the stumps to reduce the chance of this happening.

If running into the leg side and you are right-handed and need to throw as quickly as possible, we recommend getting alongside the ball, picking up in your right hand and then pivoting round your left shoulder and right foot to throw. This photo sequence shows the technique:

It is a difficult skill to master but so much quicker than getting your whole body round in the opposite direction. The crucial movement is as you come out of the rotation, you drive your left foot and left arm towards your chosen target stumps, as this will terminate your rotation momentum. As with any throw, take a split second to get a solid base, and drive towards the target.

For opportunities on the other side of the wicket, you can still pick up with your right hand, set yourself and then simply step and aim towards the target and throw.

In these instances, you are nearly always going for a direct hit, but it is always worth executing a one-bounce throw into the stumps in case you miss, then the bowler or fielder can collect and attempt the run out themselves. Remember to listen for any communication from your fielders.

Whenever executing an overarm throw at the stumps, if time permits, try to throw the ball in a cross-seam position rather than an upright seam position. This will ensure that the ball does not swing and miss the stumps. Although the throwing distances will generally be shorter than a normal outfielder, hence less distance for the ball to swing, throwing cross-seam is to be encouraged if possible. Once collected, the ball is quickly rotated in the throwing hand until the cross-seam grip is felt. The ball can then be thrown to execute the run out.

Note for coaches

There is a specific drill to practise this skill in Chapter 9. It is also advantageous to let your wicketkeeper get involved in fielding drills occasionally, especially if it is skyers or run outs. It allows them to work on the two skills and also gives them some variety in their training, which they will certainly enjoy.

Sliding retrieve

Sliding happens a lot in all forms of the game but particularly in T20 cricket where batsmen are pinching a run and you need to slide and throw. It is important to make sure your throwing technique is good.

TOM MOORES

When chasing down a ball where the fielder is directly behind its rolling trajectory, most modern-day players execute a sliding retrieve. This enables the fielder to get down to the ball very quickly and to jump back up and throw with equal speed. This method of chase, retrieve and throw can be adopted by the wicketkeeper as long as they have light pads that are not bulky.

Often in professional matches you see the wicketkeepers wearing their pads beneath their trousers, particularly in limited-overs cricket, which enables them to slide with greater efficiency.

For the purpose of explanation, we will assume the keeper is a right-handed thrower. As they approach the rolling ball, they position themselves to the right side of the ball, i.e., the ball is on the left side of their body. Whilst keeping low, the keeper jumps to the side of the ball, landing on the side of their left thigh and buttock, the left leg being bent. The keeper should try to slide on the side of the thigh and buttock, not jump directly on to them from a high position. At the same time, the right leg is kept as straight as possible, pointing out in front of the keeper. The arrangement of bent left leg and straight right leg should take the shape of a number four. Whilst sliding, the right foot should then be pressed into the ground to act as a brake, stopping the slide and enabling the keeper to jump up and execute the throw. It is important that you regularly practise this sliding retrieve. Left handed stop and throw demonstrated here (left-handed stop and throw shown):

From behind the wicket

The other type of run out that occasionally occurs if a game gets really close is when you are stood back and the batter tries to steal a single through to you. Here you are nearly always looking at a direct hit at the striker's end stumps. Whether this is overarm or underarm will be determined by how far back you are and also which method you have the most confidence in to hit the stumps with your gloves still on. Most would say underarm but practise both. Additionally, practise whipping off your throwing-arm glove and throw as quickly and as accurately as possible.

There is a method for underarm throwing that you will have been previously taught, so it is worth recapping here. Similar to an overarm throw, you should step towards the stumps with your left foot and aim with your left arm. This makes sure that your feet, hips and shoulders are aligned with the stumps and your throwing arm will come through straight towards them. Crucially, this movement will also give you more momentum and power in the throw.

Note for coaches

When you are simply hitting some catches, why not have a set of stumps set up slightly off to an angle and ask the wicketkeeper to try to hit them with an underarm throw after each catch? If they need to dive to take the catch, see if they can hit from a one-knee position.

Run outs – fielders' returns

There will be many chances during a season for you to effect a run out from a fielder's throw-in, many of which will not be on target. If a throw is wide, try to leave one foot by or close to the stumps so it is easier to get yourself and the ball back to them. Keep a strong wide base with bent knees, which will enable you to move quickly back to the stumps. Remember Jos Buttler's run out to win the World Cup!

Should you stand in front of the stumps and give behind you to effect the run out, or stand behind the stumps to take there, and then go for the run out? The answer depends on how much you have practised each option, and where the ball has gone in the field. If the ball is inside the fielding ring, the fielder may well need to go for a direct hit – in which case you need to get behind the wicket and not impede that opportunity. If hit into the outfield, it is less likely that the fielder will be going for a direct hit and you could come in front.

Standing in front definitely cuts off some time when compared with waiting behind the stumps but is a harder skill to learn, and there is a danger of treading on the stumps.

Technically you are also not standing exactly in front of the wickets either; you are at an angle, which means you have a better understanding of where the stumps are than if you have your back to them. It also produces a more dynamic position for you to move in any direction should the throw be wide.

During the course of an innings, the fielding team will adopt different strategies regarding the throws to the wicketkeeper. When the ball is new and hard, it is advisable to throw the ball on the full back to the keeper. This ensures minimal contact with the ground, which allows the ball to stay new and hard for longer, whilst it is in the hands of the quicker opening bowlers. The keeper should endeavour to take every throw on the full, so they must be very positive with their footwork when tidying up poor throws. A wet outfield may also be a reason for keeping the ball up. Eventually the new-ball bowlers will be replaced by slower seamers and spinners.

This is usually the time to start throwing in bounce throws to the keeper. Every impact into the ground helps with softening, degrading and ageing the ball. A softer ball is harder to hit for six than a hard one! The format of the game will dictate how long these strategies take place for; hence they are different for Test matches, four-day matches, 50-over matches and T20s. Fielders should be throwing the ball in with a cross-seam grip where possible. Often in a T20 the fielding team will opt for a bounce throw right from the start.

Note for coaches

When doing a fielding drill with wicketkeepers collecting the returns, ask them to simulate taking the bails off each time and emphasise the speed of doing it. Set up a flexi-stump for them to stand behind and, if it is right over the top, they simply knock the stump with the ball in the gloves. If it is wide or high, ask them to have a shy instead. Over the course of the practice, they will have opportunities from an array of different angles and body positions. Additionally, ask them to take some in front of the stumps, emphasising a give behind them into the stumps.

Stumping off a wide delivery

Remember that a wicketkeeper can stump a batter off a wide delivery. Therefore, it is recommended that you actually complete a stumping attempt if possible, as the batter may have wandered out of the crease in attempting to hit the ball. In limited-overs cricket, where wides, particularly leg-side wides, are more common, it is worth taking the bails off every time.

Stumping the striking batter's runner

Occasionally one of the batters will be injured and have a runner. When the injured batter is on strike, the runner must stand square on, opposite the square leg umpire. You need to be aware if the runner is attempting to gain an advantage by leaving their ground before the batter has played a shot. As you will be watching the ball, it is best to ask another player close by if they can spot this. If they can, then it is time to speak to the captain about formulating a plan with the bowler to run the runner out.

If the runner is out of their ground when you take the ball and then you take the bails off, they are run out. (Sorry – this does not count as a stumping!) Therefore, you can formulate a plan with the captain and bowler to deliberately bowl a ball that the batter is unlikely to hit so that you can take it and get the bails off. As you still need to be near the stumps to do this quickly, the best option, if the batter is playing well on the off side, is down the leg side, but on a good length or just back of a good length at normal pace so it is relatively easy to take. Stay relaxed and ready, and hopefully you can take it and effect the dismissal for your team!

Already broken stumps dismissal

Another form of dismissal can take place if for some reason the stumps have already been broken, with the bails dislodged. This could be from a previous run-out throw attempt, the wind blowing them off or if the keeper has accidentally knocked them off. In this situation, if the ball comes back to the keeper for a run out, the keeper must firstly take the ball, and then whilst still holding the ball in either hand, they must pull one of the stumps completely out of the ground or knock stump completely out of the ground with ball in hand. This is a rare form of dismissal, but a good keeper will have knowledge of this potential wicket opportunity.

It is essential that all wicketkeepers familiarise themselves with the MCC Laws of Cricket, particularly the laws that specifically refer to the involvement of the wicketkeeper, including wicket-taking opportunities, penalty runs and rule infringements, etc.

Jos Buttler's superb run out in the final of the 2019 World Cup.

SIX
THE MENTAL ASPECTS OF WICKETKEEPING

If you miss a catch or stumping it is important to move on quickly. It is gone and the key is to focus on the next ball. The quicker you move on, the sooner the team will forget about it.

PETER MOORES

The most important aspect of wicketkeeping is the mental side. The best wicketkeepers are able to intensify their concentration for each ball at the critical time, in other words switch on and switch off.

JACK RUSSELL

The majority of chances that wicketkeepers miss are not because of poor technique or lack of practice, it is because they were simply not mentally prepared and they reacted late to the opportunity. Often, they mentally freeze and tense up once they realise there is a chance coming their way. It is therefore essential to be mentally prepared for a chance every ball of the match, right from the first ball to the last ball of the innings, just as a batter needs to concentrate on every ball of their innings.

Like any other skill, mental skills can be worked on and improved. This will improve naturally as you become a more experienced cricketer.

Pre-match nerves

The most important thing to remember is that every player will experience some nerves pre-match or pre-innings, whether this is a batter walking out to the middle, a bowler at the top of their mark or the wicketkeeper ready to take the first ball of the game. Butterflies are natural and you can make them work for you if you can channel them in the right way to get you fired up and ready. They help get the adrenaline pumping around the body. Just by understanding that everyone has them and it is a natural process for the body and mind will help you deal with them if and when they occur.

It is important that whenever you feel nervous to focus on your breathing, taking the form of long, controlled inhalation of air. This will help you relax and take your mind off what it is you are nervous about. It is also important to reframe any negative thoughts. You may think something along the lines of, 'I hope he doesn't edge the first ball, I'm not ready,' and change it to 'I really hope he edges the first ball, I can make a name for myself early in the match.' Anything you can do internally or externally to think positively about situations will help relax you. A relaxed state of mind will give you the greatest opportunity to keep well.

Concentration

Concentration is the most important mental aspect for me.
Because if you don't concentrate in the last over in the day
and that low nick comes, you won't go for it. This is why
it's so important to switch off in between deliveries.

BEN DUCKETT

The key to concentrating for long periods of time, perhaps a full day depending on the level you are playing, is to actually only concentrate for very short periods. You only need to have a high level of concentration from when the bowler starts running in to when you have taken the ball, or the batter has hit it. Some wicketkeepers only really get to a sharp focus as the bowler enters their delivery stride. This will be around five to ten seconds per delivery. In contrast, in between this time you need to mentally relax, unless there is an opportunity to effect a run out. In other words, you need to mentally 'switch off' before 'switching on' again for the next delivery.

You may do this naturally in part already, but many wicketkeepers also have physical and mental cues just like a batter has to switch off and then back on again between deliveries. A common cue after taking the ball and moving it on to another fielder is to remake your mark, whether that is stood up or back. This is your physical cue to mentally relax. When the bowler reaches the top of their mark you can re-mark the spot again, this being your cue to ramp up your concentration and focus.

It does not have to be making a mark on the ground; some keepers adjust their pads, push their gloves together, or even verbally say something as a physical/mental cue. Whatever works well for you. It is a very personal stimulator.

Chatting with your slips is a great way to switch off in between balls. It does not have to be cricket-related, it can be absolutely anything – sport, food, nights out, etc. It is an opportunity to relax, have a laugh and have fun. It makes the day go faster and keeps you alert and in love with the job you are doing. Do not over-think, as this is very tiring. You have to love being a keeper.

A high level of physical fitness will also help you maintain concentration and focus throughout a full innings. Being physically tired will definitely be detrimental to your powers of focus and concentration. The less physically tired you are the more likely you will be able to maintain a high level of focus for each delivery throughout the innings/day's play.

The last 45 minutes of a full day's fielding, or the last ten overs of a 50-over match can be times when you are tired both physically and mentally. This period is when you are most vulnerable. To counter this, acknowledge it and rev yourself up with new positive energy, really convincing yourself that a dismissal is coming. Lift yourself and the team. Most keepers tend to be perfectionists, so be aware of this vulnerable period and come up with a game plan to counter it, thus reducing the possibility of missing a chance and keeping your confidence intact.

We talk more about fitness in Chapter 9.

Keeping your physical fitness to the highest level is vital for concentration. Check at the end of each session that you are as alert to take the ball as you were at the start of the session.

ALAN KNOTT

Mentally prepared for a chance every ball

Is it possible to be mentally prepared for a chance every ball? The answer is yes, but it is very challenging. The flatter the wicket and the more a batter is well set increases the challenge, because you may not have even taken a ball for several overs, let alone looking like a chance is coming your way.

The likelihood of you being mentally prepared for a chance are enhanced when the ball is doing something, either swinging, seaming or turning square. You always feel you are in the game and you might get an opportunity. The anticipation of an imminent chance unfolding keeps your focus and concentration high.

The ultimate mindset you should strive for is not being surprised when the batter edges the ball or just misses it. You should have prepared yourself by visualising this occurrence, mentally anticipating this dismissal opportunity. With good visualisation you will negate the possibility of a late reaction if a difficult chance is presented. You will be mentally prepared to react, and if you have the technique and confidence gained from regular practice, you will most likely pull the dismissal off. You should expect to receive every ball that is bowled to you and anticipate them edging it!

A good way to test yourself, mainly stood up to the wicket, is to ask yourself in practice and even matches whether you would have taken the ball? Were your gloves in line with the ball if the batter had missed it? If the answer is yes, then you did not mentally relax and expect the batter to hit the ball.

Note for coaches

To improve concentration, initiate practice where most balls you feed/hit are straight at the keeper, occasionally introducing a wider delivery. By incorporating this surprise delivery, you will help develop the right mental mindset to always be ready. It is also essential that a wicketkeeper keeps in the nets to the spinners and medium-pace bowlers. They do not always like it because they may not take many deliveries, but it is an important part of developing the right mental mindset. You can also instruct the batter to deliberately miss the ball once every two overs, thus assessing whether the keeper was ready or not. This may culminate in a potential stumping opportunity too. Do not be shy of stopping the bowler letting go of the ball to see what the keeper's balance and head position are like on release. You probably do this for a batter occasionally, so it is essential you do this for wicketkeepers also.

Self-talk

Self-talk is the art of either outwardly verbalising or internally using key words to ensure you remain focused. It is very important that this self-talk is positive, heightening concentration and focus, and not negative, which can make you tense up if a dismissal opportunity comes along.

You can even use self-talk as a cue to switch back on when the bowler turns at the top of their mark. It is another simple method of ensuring you are mentally alert for every ball delivered.

Note for coaches

At some stage you have probably discussed self-talk with a batter. The most common phrase used is 'watch the ball'. Encourage your wicketkeepers to do the same and discover a prompting phrase that works for them. 'Watch the ball' is fine. 'My ball' is also a good one, or a simple 'come on' at times where they feel focus is diminishing.

Switching concentration off between deliveries can help, but make sure you have a way to switch back on. Even if it means shouting at yourself, or in your mind.
ALAN KNOTT

Fear of failure

As with batting, one of the most mentally inhibiting aspects of wicketkeeping, manifested when not reacting or tensing up when a chance comes, is the fear of failing to take the opportunity. Have you ever had a sudden rush of nervousness when a batter runs down the wicket when you are stood up? That nervousness is your response to the realisation that a potential stumping is about to take place.

It is so important that you turn any negative thoughts into positive ones. For example, instead of thinking, 'He might run down the wicket and give me a stumping chance,' think, 'I hope he does run down the wicket and gives me a stumping.' You are flipping a potentially nervous moment into a very positive one where you are looking forward to an opportunity coming your way.

The other key is to ensure you practise regularly. The more you practise and the more it is match-realistic, the more confident you will be for the opportunities presented in a match. This increased confidence will reduce your nerves, thus lessening the associated negative thoughts.

However, at some stage, no matter how much natural ability you have, and no matter how good your practice and preparation has been, you will make a mistake and put a chance down. Everyone makes mistakes, no one is infallible. Every wicketkeeper interviewed for this book has missed several chances throughout their careers. Mistakes are inevitable, so you need to have a coping strategy and be mentally resilient. We have discussed how a wicketkeeper can suddenly energise a side by pulling off something brilliant, but conversely it can also go very quiet in the field when the wicketkeeper fluffs a chance.

Missing a dismissal opportunity is the hardest thing to deal with as a wicketkeeper. It's far easier said than done but you have to put it behind you and focus on the next delivery. If it affects you it could result in another mistake. Every wicketkeeper makes mistakes, so try and put it behind you.

BEN DUCKETT

So, if you accept the fact that occasionally you will make a mistake, you are already halfway to being able to move on positively should this happen during a match, or even in training. Moving on quickly is vital, as *it is always the next ball that counts*. Tell yourself that dropping catches is part of being a wicketkeeper so that the pressure comes off and you play in a more relaxed state of mind. Park it and move on.

You always need to turn any negative thoughts into positive ones. You may feel that you do not want another opportunity to come your way for a while. Flip this on its head and say to yourself, 'I hope another chance comes my way; it will be the best catch I've ever taken.'

And it could be the very next ball that the opportunity arises. A low point can turn to a high point very quickly. This is crucial if you make a mistake early in an innings. You cannot undertake the next 50 overs or the day's play dwelling on it, hoping a chance does not come your way. Reflection on what went wrong can take place at the end of the day's play, match, or even better the next time you practise, when any emotions from the game have disappeared. Just like a batter playing and missing or being hit on the head by a bouncer. That was the last ball, the next one is the one that matters.

Aim to be able to take the hard knocks and the disappointments and get ready for the next ball.
JACK RUSSELL

An important part of being a wicketkeeper is to have a person who can act as a point of reference when you think your performance levels are dropping. This could be a coach, current or old, or another wicketkeeper. In the team dynamic, there are groups of batters, bowlers and all-rounders. They very often chat amongst themselves, discussing their particular performances, sharing advice, etc. There is only normally one keeper in the team, so they generally do not have anyone to discuss their performances with. In this case, it is vital that they can use someone for advice and encouragement. Keepers regularly chat with their opposite number after matches, so this is a good starting point. A coach who has experience of keeping is the ideal preference, as they may be able to offer advice or work through any issues directly with you at a training session. It is also great to share your successes with this person. This is as relevant to a young player as it is to an experienced one. At the time of writing, there are currently three full-time wicketkeepers in the England team!

The reader is encouraged to look for further information on the mental aspects of sport and sport psychology.

SEVEN
OTHER ROLES OF
A WICKETKEEPER

It is vital that the wicketkeeper sets a good tone for the team
with strong body language and offers advice to bowlers and captains.

DAVID RIPLEY

Wicketkeepers' primary roles are to catch the ball, effect dismissals and limit byes, but to fulfil the role of wicketkeeper completely, a lot more will be expected of you. There are an extensive variety of ways that you can affect the course of the game, from helping the captain with the field, tips for the bowlers, identifying weaknesses in a batter's technique, energising and encouraging the fielders, tidying-up returns from the outfield, getting in the batter's ear and making sure the slips are standing in the correct position. You may also be the captain of the team and have to make the bulk of the tactical decisions. If you do these jobs well, you will be enhancing overall team performance. However, the overriding consideration is that you perform your primary roles well. The rest are all the extras, the icing on the cake that you bring to the team to improve overall performance.

Energising the team

A wicketkeeper needs the ability to be able to stay upbeat for long periods of time. The wicketkeeper is the focal point of the fielding unit and his mood often reflects how well a team is fielding at any given time.

PETER MOORES

Nearly all captains and coaches like their wicketkeepers to be the engine room of the team. If you perform your primary roles well you will already be doing this in part, but during the period where you have mentally relaxed between deliveries, there is plenty of time for you to offer some words of encouragement to fielders and the bowler. The wicketkeeper is expected to be the constant voice keeping everyone motivated and upbeat. This is especially important if the batting team is on top, and you should look to double your efforts in this situation. It is very easy to stay focused and energised as a team when wickets are falling regularly, not as easy when there has not been a wicket for 30 overs. This is the time for you to be the motivator.

As a team you always want the batter to feel they are on their own, one against 11, so the wicketkeeper has an important role to play in that regard. Throughout any innings, the wicketkeeper is generally the closest fielder to the batter, particularly when stood up to the wicket, so the role here is considerable.

In addition to being vocal, there are other ways you can energise a team, such as getting up to the stumps after every ball so that the fielder can throw the ball in to you. The very movement displays energy and keeps the fielder involved by having to throw the ball in to you, and the slips moving round to back up the throw. This also has the added benefit of bringing you closer to the batter, allowing them to hear your comments regarding another dot ball. Even if you are simply encouraging the team, you are closer to them, increasing the loudness of your voice, compared to when you are standing back on your mark.

During a match, all captains will have an eye on their team's over rate, and you can contribute to the change between overs being as swift as possible. Aim to be the first through to your mark at the end of the over, and by verbalising encouragement for your team-mates to do the same, you are displaying energy and subsequently energising the team.

Whilst you would expect your fielding team-mates to be well drilled in backing up throws, etc., the keeper should always be looking to call the fielders in to back up both sets of stumps appropriately. Encouraging fielders when they are chasing a ball, or applauding great stops, great throws, etc., all helps with lifting the team. Remember the phrase: 'Are you putting into the team pot or are you taking from it?' In plumbing terms: 'Are you a drain or a radiator?'

When stood up to the wicket you can display a lot of energy by what we will term 'controlling your area'. Aim to think of any area around the batter within a ten-yard radius as yours. The ball will often be played softly by the batter or hit a pad and trickle away. Be quick to react, whip your glove off if necessary and look busy. As well as showing the batters that you are alert to them sneaking a single, you are simply being very active and energetic, and this can rub off on the team. Lead by example.

Remember that you need to be ready for the next delivery and fully focused to do your primary role by the time the bowler reaches the top of their mark again. Energising the team is important but not at the expense of missing a dismissal opportunity.

A wicketkeeper is the heartbeat of the team, the drummer of the band, and it is important that they set the tone and control the tempo in the field. They also have the best view to judge angles because you can see from the batsman's perspective. This will improve with experience.

TIM MOORES

Field placings and helping the captain and bowler

I really enjoyed helping the captain out with angles for fielders and effectively having a vice-captain role with tactics, as you have the best view of the game.

BEN DUCKETT

It is nearly impossible for the captain to have an eye on ten outfielders each delivery. You have an important role to play in checking angles and getting fielders into the right position, including the slips if they are in.

When you are up to the stumps, you are in a similar position to the batter, so you can literally see the field as they see it. You are well placed to judge whether fielders in the ring are tight enough to save the single, outfielders are saving two, and that they are at the correct angle in between the fielders in the circle. Astute field positioning will save your team runs and increase the chances of run outs.

When judging the positioning of slips it is important that this is made from your final set position, not from where you trigger from, should you have a trigger. To position first slip you need to work out how far you could dive to take a one-handed catch if it were dropping short of first slip, and it was edged from the line of the stumps, no wider. Whilst you are building the experience to judge this, you can work it out in practice by lying down full-stretch with one arm out, measured from your final set position. Where your outstretched hand finishes is the line for first slip. They then need to be a long step back from there to allow you and second slip to move in front of them if required.

Second slip then moves into position, level with your final set position marks, ensuring they will be stood level with you once you are in your ready position.

Angles of slips will change for different bowlers. If you are keeping to a left-arm over-the-wicket bowler, you would be standing quite wide to get a clear view of the bowler. If they then decide to bowl around the wicket, you would reposition yourself to be straighter. It is important that the slips are also repositioned, ensuring a chance does not get through the catching cordon.

As a wicketkeeper you are well placed to get a good look at a batter's technique – how they grip the bat, where they stand in relation to the stumps, open stance, closed stance, etc. This information can be relayed to the captain and bowler if you feel a batter may have a weakness in a particular area. Between you, you can formulate a plan to get the batter out or restrict their scoring.

I will ask wicketkeepers to identify whether a batsman is walking or overbalancing, therefore giving a chance of a stumping or lbw. I will also ask him to look at a batsman's grip. Is he more a leg-side or off-side player? Does he hit it square and behind the wicket or down the ground? And is there a difference in that between pace and spin?

DAVID RIPLEY

For example, if a batter's head falls over to the off side at the bowler's point of release, they may fall across their stumps, making them a prime candidate for lbw or chipping the ball in the air, etc. The bowler could then be advised to bowl straight and full to effect an lbw or make relevant field changes. Assessment of a batter's equipment can also give an indication of how they play. If the batter's bat grip is worn at the top, this could indicate that they are a top-hand player, and subsequently, if the grip is worn at the bottom, this may indicate a bottom-handed batter. Field placings can again be repositioned accordingly. Similarly, if one of the batter's gloves is worn out more than the other, this may again indicate their dominant hand preference. Red ball marks on batters' gloves generally indicate that they may struggle against fast, short-pitched bowling. Finally, if a batter's front pad is covered in red ball marks, this may indicate that they are susceptible to full, straight deliveries.

Additionally, as the wicketkeeper changes ends after each over, they are in a position to overhear the batters' conversation, possibly determining their tactical game plan.

Bowlers also like feedback. They may ask you how it is hitting the gloves or whether there is much movement. Although you will be watching the ball, you may be able to pass on some small technical observations as well, which can improve their performance in that innings.

Mentally distracting the batter

Although we would not advocate spending the majority of your time between deliveries sledging the opposition's batters, a lot of wicketkeepers do like to talk to them. The reason is to break their concentration and get them out of their batting bubble to increase the chances of getting them out. As you are up to the stumps a lot, you are better placed than other fielders to execute this strategy. This should never be personal, but can be related to the match situation or a flaw in their technique, etc. Any form of distraction can break their focus. Very often, continued exuberant encouragement of bowlers and fielders can satisfy this.

Players and coaches should always have the MCC Laws of Cricket and the MCC Spirit of Cricket uppermost in their minds and should ensure that they stay within these boundaries of behaviour whilst on the field of play, additionally setting a good example to younger players.

Every player is different in their approach to this side of the game and it should not be done if it detracts from your own performance in any way. If it does, then it is definitely not worth doing and you should focus your energies on lifting your team-mates instead of thinking of the next thing to say to the batter.

Firstly, you have to make sure your game is in order and consistently to a high standard before you start playing mind games with the opposition, otherwise things may come back to haunt you.

JACK RUSSELL

Desirable personality traits

Wicketkeepers are now seen as all-round players who need to be able to contribute with the bat as well as with the gloves on.

PETER MOORES

Most wicketkeepers in this era are all-rounders, who have a role to play in the top seven of the batting order. However, if you are not batting that high at the moment, and are more of a wicketkeeper, it is possible to improve your batting skills as you will have good hand-eye co-ordination and agile footwork. Similarly, it is possible to turn a batter who is a good catcher of the ball into a high-level wicketkeeper.

The best position for you to bat as a wicketkeeper is down to personal preference. If you are an opening bat and that is your preference, then stick with this as long as your fitness levels are high. Yes, you may be physically tired after 50 overs in the field, or a full day if you are already playing multi-day cricket, but your eye is also in as you have had balls coming at you for three-plus hours. You will be seeing the ball well! If you have mastered the switching on/off skill well, you should not be too mentally jaded either.

If you are not an opener, it is advisable to bat no higher than five. This will give you time to have a genuine rest, both mentally and physically, before going out to bat. Batting at No. 3 or 4 is difficult because you start to relax and unwind at the start of the fielding innings, but you can also be in very early and have to then get yourself going again. It is easier to get straight back out there or give yourself a genuine break. Everyone is different though, so if you are highly successful batting at No. 3 and wicketkeeping, then stick with it. The great Sri Lankan player, Kumar Sangakkara, managed this for years.

If you bat in the lower-middle order, you should have had a decent rest, but your role as a batter becomes different. The key thing here is to get the runs when your team really needs them; that is, when the top order has not fired or you need to see your team over the finishing line. Aim to become known as the 'finisher' and walking off with a stump at the end of the innings.

The biggest challenge in modern professional cricket is balancing batting preparation and wicketkeeping preparation. Chris Read's advice to me was to do equal amounts of both disciplines. I am usually the last one out of the changing room and have to train for longer than the other players to fit it all in.

TOM MOORES

Your role as a batter

Discussing personality traits is always interesting as not everyone is an outgoing, drum-banging type personality, but there is a need to keep body language strong and offering advice to bowlers and captains is important. It is also important that the wicketkeeper sets the tone for the rest of the team.

DAVID RIPLEY

We have previously highlighted how important a wicketkeeper's role is and how much you are involved in the game each ball. With this is mind, wicketkeeping certainly suits certain personalities and below is a list of desirable personality traits. It is unlikely you will have them all and certainly do not worry if you do not at this stage. As with technique, these traits can be worked on and improved upon, though remember, everyone is different!

• Brave – It takes courage to keep to fast bowling, top-spinners and stood up to seam bowling. Your hands take a pounding. Your fingers can get broken and when you are stood up you can get deflections off bat and stumps into your body. Enjoy these challenges and do not let them dishearten you. Many wicketkeepers keep playing even if they have broken a finger.

• Determined – We have discussed the importance of being mentally and physically prepared for a dismissal opportunity. You need determination to want to affect the game and influence its result.

• Resilient – There will be times when things do not go as well as you would want them to and perhaps a chance has gone down. You need personal resilience to get through these times and maintain or maximise your performance levels.

• Optimist – With a game that is as mentally challenging as cricket, it is important to have that feeling that today is going to be your day. Even if the last match did not go well, it is so important to promote a mentally positive outlook and look forward to each match, session and delivery.

• Upbeat – Remember your role as the team energiser. Aim to be busy, energetic and bubbly. If you are constantly showing signs of frustration – kicking the turf or hurling the ball into the ground – this is negative body language, which will rub off on the team. Bowlers will not be particularly confident that you are in the right frame of mind to take a catch either.

• Honest – It is essential that you reflect upon your performance objectively and honestly, whether this is self-reflection or with the captain or coach. Remember, this should take place at training or after the match, not during the match itself.

• Hard-working – Wicketkeeping is both physically and mentally tiring so you need to enjoy hard work and have a high level of personal fitness.

• Patient – There will be times when not much is happening and you may not be involved as much as you would like to be. You need to be patient and ready for when an opportunity presents itself. Stay engaged and focused – there may be a dismissal opportunity next ball!

I believe you've got to be a team man as a wicketkeeper and self-sufficient and self-driven. There is only one wicketkeeper in a team, and you don't have someone else doing your discipline, like the batsmen and bowlers have, who they can bounce ideas off. There is a need to be strong mentally and deal with the bad days and still be a giver to the team.

TOM MOORES

It is interesting to note how the wicketkeeper's role has changed over the years, particularly with the more recent popularity of 50-over and T20 cricket. Generally, in the past, a wicketkeeper was selected for their high level of keeping skills, and their batting was a secondary requirement. Many keepers batted later in the batting order. Nowadays, this role has somewhat been reversed, with their potential as a batter possibly outweighing their wicketkeeping abilities. It is true that you do improve the more you keep, so even those keepers selected for their batting, will improve their keeping skills. Wicketkeepers are all-rounders, so it is vital that they work on the weaker side of their game too.

With the popularity of T20 cricket around the world, wicketkeepers selected on their keeping abilities could be making a comeback. A reason for this is the short length of a T20 innings. Generally, teams can carry a high-quality keeper who may not be the greatest batter. This keeper has the potential to earn wickets for their team, either by consistently taking great catches and making stumpings or by standing up to the wicket more often, creating pressure, thus removing the batter's option of safely leaving the crease to manufacture shots. There are many more spin bowlers in T20 cricket now, particularly wrist spinners, with many opening the bowling, so it is essential that they are backed up by a highly skilled keeper. A great keeper could gain their side so many more important wickets and have a massive influence on the match outcome. On the batting side, it would not matter if the keeper batted at No. 11, as it is unusual for a side to lose that many wickets in T20 cricket. It would be interesting to see how much keepers like Alan Knott and Jack Russell would cost at auction for a T20 franchise today. Jack Russell was so instrumental in all the limited-over success Gloucestershire had in the 1990s.

EIGHT
LOOKING AFTER YOURSELF
(PRE-MATCH PREPARATION, FITNESS, NUTRITION, HYDRATION, SLEEP & EQUIPMENT)

Pre-match preparations are very individual, although a regular routine can help the wicketkeeper gain consistency and mentally be ready from ball one in the game. Wicketkeeping is a physically demanding job so being physically fit is very important. Power, mobility and stamina all play their part in the life of a wicketkeeper.

PETER MOORES

Pre-match preparation

You need to be ready for everything that might happen that day. If you're not, you will substantially increase the possibilities of making mistakes.

JACK RUSSELL

The most important aspect of any pre-match preparation is to feel physically and mentally prepared for the task ahead, commencing the match feeling confident about your wicketkeeping and ready from ball one. Similar to a batter looking to feel the ball coming out of the middle of the bat, to feel confident about your game as a wicketkeeper you need to feel the ball going into the gloves sweetly for a range of takes, combined with good foot movement.

How much preparation you can do before the start of play

will depend on the level you are currently playing, and when teams arrive before play is due to start. You may also be relying on your parents to get you to the match on time!

Primarily, pre-match preparation is the player's responsibility, although you need an understanding of how the coach and captain can help facilitate that. Pre-match is not the time for hard-core fitness routines and drills, as you do not want to be physically tired going into the day's play, especially if you are fielding first. It is important to conserve energy for the day ahead.

It is essential that the keeper undertakes a warm-up. This prepares the body and mind for action, by increasing blood flow, increasing heart rate and warming the muscles up. It increases the range of movement, improves body co-ordination, and switches the player on mentally for the job in hand. After the initial warm-up, a series of full-body dynamic stretches should take place, preparing the keeper for the day's play and greatly increasing injury prevention. After this warm-up period the keeper should then undertake their specific wicketkeeping routines.

A vital element in injury prevention is to undertake a warm-down at the close of play. This will involve light jogging, etc., increasing blood flow and heart rate and warming the muscles up.

A series of full-body dynamic stretches should then take place. A warm-down is essential, as it helps to reduce muscle soreness, aids recovery, helps to improve flexibility and greatly increases injury prevention. This is particularly important in multi-day cricket or if you have another match the following day.

The reader is encouraged to look for further information on the subject of warm-ups and warm-downs.

If your team is batting first, and you bat lower down the order, preparation can take place if desired but should be performed after the toss is completed. With approximately 20 minutes remaining you can take the opportunity to invest in some extra preparation, taking your rest at the commencement of your team's innings.

Ideally you want to exercise as many elements of the wicketkeeping duties that you are likely to demonstrate in the match ahead:

- Low, waist-high, above-shoulder takes
- Takes away to the right- and left-hand side of your body
- Dives to the left and right, both two- and one-handed
- Stood up to seam
- Stood up to spin
- Yorker-length and very full takes

Remember, it is essential that you also work on your batting skills, especially if you bat in the top order. If you bat lower down the order, you may have time when the top order is in to do your batting practice then. Remember, you are the engine room of the side, so aim to be at the ground early if needs be to get yourself prepared, thus setting a good tone for the team. It is essential that the wicketkeeper, through good time management, is in position to keep to the bowlers once their bowling warm-up commences.

In addition to a routine of takes, hit or thrown by a player or coach, it is essential that you take some balls from the bowlers during their warm-up. Hopefully, this can be done on the square, as this will also give you an indication of the pace and bounce in the wicket, thus an idea of how far back to stand when the match gets underway. Try to face both seam and spin, and if you can, get someone to shadow bat with a flexi-stump or some foam pipe lagging if you keep some in your kit bag. Taking yorker-length and very full underarm or overarm throws is also essential. Look to keep your eyes on the ball and your head straight and 'in there', not flinching away. A warm-up and warm-down are an essential part of your pre-match preparations.

Pre-match preparation drills are indicated in the next chapter.

Note for coaches

If possible, try to avoid using the keeper to take throws in your fielding drills. They have plenty more important keeping skills to be working on.

Routine is important. Make time for your own game as well as contributing to team stuff. Make sure you take some deliveries from the bowlers and work on your batting.

DAVID RIPLEY

Fitness

A high level of fitness is crucial for a wicketkeeper. Without it you get fatigued. With fatigue you make mistakes.

JACK RUSSELL

Hopefully, this book has emphasised the multifaceted role you have to play as a wicketkeeper. If you are also a top-order batter, you are going to need to be fit to meet the physical demands of the two roles. Remember that a high level of physical fitness will also aid concentration and the ability to maintain a sharp focus throughout the whole innings. Without a strong physique, eventually over a prolonged period of a day's play, your technique can falter.

We will assume you also have an important role to play with the bat, so you will need a broad level of all-round fitness. You will need power in your legs to move quickly, dynamically and to dive when necessary. You will need high levels of stamina to compete at a high level with both bat and ball for a full day's play. You will need speed to 'control your area' and run quickly between the wickets when batting. You need to be flexible and agile. Finally, you will need upper-body strength to hit the ball with power when you bat.

Do not focus on one area more than another, as they are all equally important. If you focus excessively on lifting weights to build strength and power, you will bulk up too much to move quickly, which will be detrimental to your energy levels for a full day's play.

It is helpful to be lean as a wicketkeeper and not carry too much bulk. Your leg weights exercise routine should consist of lower weights and higher repetitions. Although it often goes against sports science advice, your reps can be done at pace, dynamically. Imagine each rep you do is you leaping off the ground to take a high wide ball. Higher weights and lower reps build bulk, which can be detrimental to a wicketkeeper. Speed of movement should be your aim.

A strong core is very important to complement the lower-body power required, in addition to the range of movement required to be a wicketkeeper. Great core stability, coupled with a strong lower back, are essential elements for a keeper. A resistance band is often used in wicketkeeping drills, as the increased resistance improves core stability, power, speed, balance and movement technique levels. Weights can be used to add upper-body strength, but rowing and swimming are also great alternatives. They are excellent ways to enhance the leanness of your upper body, also providing a high-intensity cardio workout.

For stamina, there is nothing better than getting miles in your legs. Unless you have knee, back or ankle issues, running is the best way to build your stamina and endurance. You could use a slow, long-distance run as the initial part of your workout routine prior to commencing your weights. Make sure you do a long stretch after your run as this will help your flexibility. It is also important to keep stretching in breaks between sets when doing your weights routine.

To improve agility, it is important to do exercises that get you moving in multiple directions. Ladders and cone work are the most common, and any drills that involve speed of movement will help you. Try to do some when you are chasséing, like you would do when keeping. There are some great examples you can use in the next chapter.

Note for coaches

To emphasise how fit a wicketkeeper has to be, we have produced a very general assessment of a keeper's potential movements during a 50-over match, culminating in a rough guide as to the distance travelled whilst fielding.

For this example, we will assume that there will be 30 overs of seam and 20 overs of spin.

The keeper will be stood back to all three seamers and will be jogging between overs from one end to the other. The set-up position for the seamers will be ten yards behind the stumps. Finally, whilst keeping to the seamers, the keeper will run up to the stumps on three occasions during the over.

Seam bowling – The keeper will swap ends 30 times, jogging a distance of 42 yards. They will sprint up to the stumps 90 times.

Spin bowling – The keeper will swap ends 20 times, jogging a distance of 22 yards

Therefore, the total distance covered is: 30x42 + 90x10 + 20x22 = 2,600 yards (1.47 miles or 2.37 kilometres)

Of this, 900 yards (0.51 miles or 984 metres) will be sprinted when running up to the stumps. That is the equivalent of ten 100-metre sprint races

(Conversion criteria: 1 yard = 0.914 metres; 1 mile = 1,760 yards or 1.61 kilometres)

This example does not take account of any additional balls faced emanating from wides or no balls.

In addition to the base datum of 50 overs, variables such as the heat the game is played in and the concentration required to perform this role only exacerbate the importance of having a high level of fitness. Remember, the keeper will also be batting!

Fitness is massively important. You have to be on it every single ball of the day. There might be one opportunity in the last over of the day which could affect the result of the game.

BEN DUCKETT

Nutrition

The following text provides a general outline on the subject of nutrition. For more expansive knowledge the reader should consult literature beyond the scope of this book.

Cricket is a sport that involves bursts of intense energy over a long duration. This principle also applies to wicketkeeping. To ensure a keeper has enough energy stores available to meet the demands of their role, it is essential that they have a basic knowledge of the importance of eating food that will deliver energy throughout the day's play.

The food sources needed can be divided into the following categories: carbohydrates, proteins, fats, vitamins and fibre.

Carbohydrates
Carbohydrates can be divided into two forms: starches (complex carbohydrates) and sugars (simple carbohydrates). During the bursts of intense activity, it is the carbohydrates that provide the essential energy source. They should form the major part of a wicketkeeper's diet, approximately 50–60 per cent. They are stored in the muscles as glycogen, which is depleted rapidly during exercise, so it is essential that stores are kept topped up. Lack of glycogen in the muscles results in fatigue.

Good sources of complex carbohydrates are: potatoes, pasta, rice, bread, porridge, cereals, baked beans, nuts, fresh fruit, dried fruit, etc. These carbohydrates are great at releasing glycogen to the muscles over a long period of time.

Good sources of simple carbohydrates are: sugars, confectionery, jams, ice cream, etc. These carbohydrates are great at releasing glycogen to the muscles via a quick energy burst.

It is important to remember how long it takes glycogen to be produced for each type of carbohydrate.

Proteins
Protein should only form approximately 10–15 per cent of a keeper's energy intake, and is found in meats, fish, eggs, yoghurts, milk, cheese, dairy products, nuts, beans, etc.

Fats
A keeper should try to regulate their dietary fat content to

no more than 35 per cent of their total energy intake. Fat is extremely high in energy but is not very suitable for the time durations encountered in a cricket match. Foods that are high in fat are biscuits, chocolate, butter, mayonnaise, eggs, cheese, fried foods, etc.

Vitamins

Most vitamins are found in a balanced diet, but many can be found in vitamin supplements. Vitamin D can also be found in natural sunlight in addition to natural food sources.

Fibre

Whilst fibre is not an energy source, it is essential for digestive health and regular bowel movements, and controls blood sugar levels. Foods high in fibre are wholegrain breakfast cereals, wholewheat pasta, wholegrain bread, fruit, vegetables, peas, beans, nuts, potatoes with skin, etc.

I don't have a big heavy meal during the day. Breakfast is important. I like porridge and eggs to give me energy. I will have a light lunch along the lines of chicken and salad. For tea, just very light snacks.

TOM MOORES

The best way of sustaining the relevant energy levels is to eat small regular meals, ensuring that glycogen levels are replenished fully. Digestion of food takes approximately two to three hours, so timing this intake is very important. There is a good reason why it is said that breakfast is the most important meal of the day. Small regular meals also mean that you will never be too full at any point during the day. If you play cricket with a lunch break it is easy to overeat in terms of quantity and the wrong type of food. This can have a negative effect on performance and mindset by going into the next session feeling lethargic and uncomfortable.

After a match or practice session it is important to replenish your energy stores. This not only replaces the energy sources used up but helps in the body's recovery. Eating a high-carbohydrate meal within two hours of exercise is essential, as this is the most receptive time for storing glycogen.

Hydration

The following text provides a general outline on the subject of hydration. For more expansive knowledge the reader should consult literature beyond the scope of this book.

It is critically important that a wicketkeeper guards against the effects of dehydration. Wearing inners, gloves, pads and a helmet means that a keeper is highly susceptible to dehydration.

We have previously estimated the distances and intensities involved in a 50-over match, so it is essential that a player remains fully hydrated, as water plays a crucial role in regulating body temperature.

Water and minerals are lost through sweating, so it is essential these are replaced. Crucially, every kilogram of loss in body weight through sweating equates to a litre of body fluid lost.

Performance is impaired if dehydration is 2 per cent of body weight, and if it reaches 5 per cent, this means that the body's capacity for work reduces by 30 per cent. Players can easily lose two to five litres of fluid during a game. Dehydration will produce deterioration in co-ordination and decision-making, and an increase in fatigue. An increase in fatigue will, in turn, affect your ability to concentrate and stay focused.

Dehydration can cause decreased sweat rates, decreased heat dissipation, increased core temperatures, increased blood pressure and the increased rate of depleting glycogen stores. To avoid this, it is essential that players drink on a regular basis throughout training and matchdays. A good rule of thumb is to endeavour to drink between every 20–40 minutes.

Coaches and players should ensure that plenty of fluids are available before, during and after activity. If you become thirsty you are already dehydrated, so the key is to avoid this by taking regular fluid intakes. A great way of checking for dehydration is to check the colour of your urine. If it is yellow, you are already dehydrated; if it is clear, i.e., looking like water, you are hydrated. Wicketkeepers should avoid alcohol and caffeinated drinks at least 24 hours before a match, as these fluids both act as diuretics, thus promoting dehydration. Excessive alcohol consumption after a match is detrimental to the body's recovery system and can impair the following day's performance.

Symptoms of heat stress can be identified as follows: loss of co-ordination, feeling cold, dizziness, confusion and pale complexion. If a player displays these symptoms, they should be removed from the field of play immediately and appropriate medical attention sought.

Wicketkeeping in the heat

Because cricket is a summer sport, a wicketkeeper will regularly be playing and training in hot temperatures and on sunny days. We have previously mentioned the importance of avoiding dehydration, so this has even greater importance on these occasions. In addition to this, keepers can take certain measures to avoid the effects of these intense conditions. The wearing of caps and sunhats is to be encouraged, and this is essential for young players. All young wicketkeepers will be wearing helmets, so whilst this will protect most of their head from the effects of the sun, it gets extremely hot in a helmet, thus exacerbating the effect of high temperatures. A keeper also wears inners and full wicketkeeping gloves, so this also adds to their body core temperature. A keeper should be encouraged to remove their helmet and gloves regularly at appropriate intervals, to allow the free movement of fresh cooling air. This can be between every over as they swap ends if time allows.

The application of a high-protection sunscreen or barrier screen is essential, and a keeper should wear long-sleeved cotton shirts whenever possible, which also helps to protect the elbows when diving on hard ground. The use of sunglasses is also recommended, as these will lessen the negative effects of spending all day in the sun. Taking a cold shower between innings is a great way to cool down after a long period in the sun. When wicketkeepers are waiting to bat, they should endeavour to stay in the shade and keep cool as much as possible. Whilst batting, the general rules for coping with hot temperatures should apply.

Sleep

The following text provides a general outline about sleep. For more expansive knowledge the reader should consult literature beyond the scope of this book.

In addition to nutrition and hydration, another important element of a wicketkeeper's preparation is having enough sleep. Sleep is the body's natural way of recovering from the day's exertions. It is essential for our health and wellbeing, particularly in the sporting environment, and it is recommended that a minimum of eight hours' sleep is required. If this can be achieved, a keeper enhances their chances of performing well with both gloves and bat. There are several ways this can be achieved, some of which are recommended below.

Have a warm bath or shower directly before getting into bed. Refrain from using mobile phones at least 30 minutes before getting into bed and do not watch TV in bed. Keep your bedroom cool and well ventilated and sleep in fresh bed linen as often as is practically possible. Drink milk or a vitamin-fortified drink before going to sleep, avoid chocolate or cheese directly before bed and avoid a big meal late at night.

It is not just the duration of sleep that is important. There are different cycles of sleep that ensure you wake fully refreshed and ready for the day ahead. One of the most important aspects of getting a good night's sleep is routine and you should aim to go to bed the night before play at the same time as you would normally do to stick to your normal pattern.

Equipment

*When deciding on a pair of gloves, the bigger the better,
but inners need to be worn and your fingers need to
go into the end of the glove.*
DAVID RIPLEY

Buying the right equipment and looking after it is important,
and below is a list of the essentials that you will need:

- Gloves
- Inners
- Spikes
- Wicketkeeping pads
- Band-Aid tape
- Spare spikes
- Helmet
- Box
- Cap/sunhat and sunglasses

It is also worth carrying around some pipe lagging foam as well for shadow practice.

What you can afford will obviously influence your decision on the quality of these items unless you are fortunate enough to be a sponsored player. Try to buy a glove that is a size too big as well. If you do not mind the feel, it will give you a larger catching area. With gloves, it is important that they are flexible and that the main catching area of the glove is large.

Always try gloves on first and see how they fit your hands. Also, if you put your hand on top of the glove, the thumb should rest where your thumb naturally sits when your hand is open. The positioning of the thumb is important as it can restrict the size of the catching area if it is stitched into the wrong position.

PETER MOORES

Some gloves have an area cut away on the palm, and others where the thumb joint protrudes too far into the hand. Avoid these if you can. Gloves, like bats, can be knocked in, although most are quite supple on purchase. You can use a corner of a bat to 'knock in' the areas where you will be mainly taking the ball, ensuring the rubber has plenty of give in it. Throwing a ball repeatedly into the glove is another good way to knock them in. Remember, it is vitally important that you also use them in practice a few times before a match. Most wicketkeepers would keep the gloves together the opposite way around in their kit bags with their inners in between. Try to keep them as flat as possible in your kit bag. If you find a pair you love, think about getting the pimpled rubber palms re-faced when they become worn through. This is also cheaper than buying a new pair of gloves. If you can afford to, also keep a spare pair in your bag – one for matches and one for practice.

How many inners you wear will be down to personal preference and the size of your hands. If you like to have more feel, then one pair of inners is fine. The more you wear, the less feel you have of the ball. If you struggle with persistent bruising, then you may want to wear an extra pair to help cushion the ball. If you have small hands, you may want to think about an extra pair too, especially if you are using a size up in glove. A good idea is to buy the first pair, fitting correctly to your hand size, then the second pair being the next size up, fitting over the first pair. This will ensure the inners feel comfortable in your gloves.

Good quality, comfortable spiked footwear is essential, as you are going to be on your feet a lot. It is advised that you carry some spare spikes in your kit bag to replace any that wear down or come out. A full set of spikes on your footwear is important to make sure you push off when you need to, ensuring your feet do not slip. Your weight is also evenly distributed into the ground, reducing the chance of sore feet.

When assessing wicketkeeping pads, think mainly about the weight. They need to be lightweight so you can move quickly, not hindering your movement. It is vital that they are not too big for the same reason. When bent down in your stance, as long as the knee is protected, that is satisfactory. Weight is also your main consideration for your helmet as well. The lighter the better – especially if you are stood up to the wicket a lot, crouching with your head up. The ball should not be able to fit through between grill and visor.

If you do get a lot of bruising, you can buy artificial fat that you can tape on to an inner on the area where you get the bruising. This helps protect that area. Simply using tape if you cannot get hold of the artificial fat or cannot afford it will also help. Blu-Tack or Plasticine is another option. Your fingers, particularly the knuckles, can also take a pounding, so a lot of wicketkeepers like to tape their knuckles up as well.

Wicketkeeping wagon wheel assessment sheet

Opposite is a copy of an ECB wicketkeeping wagon wheel assessment sheet. This is a very useful method of assessing the current technical, physical and mental status of a wicketkeeper.

It can be completed by both the keeper and their coach, and a comparison made between the two. The sheet identifies key strengths and areas for improvement. This will then lead to an individual development plan, discussed and formulated by both individuals, based on short-term and long-term development goals. It can be updated on a regular basis to assess progress.

The concentric circles are numbered 1–10: 0 = Weak; 10 = Excellent

Each segment is shaded up to the current evaluated skill level.

WICKET KEEPING

CRICKETER:	DATE:
SQUAD:	COACH:

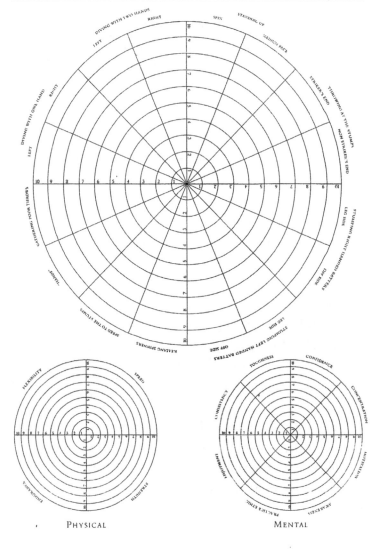

PHYSICAL

MENTAL

NINE
TRAINING DRILLS

Make practice as match real as you can. Get your bowlers to bowl as they would in a match. Preferably one bowler at a time. And practise the hard skills like taking the full driving full-length balls off the orthodox spinner. Perfect practice makes perfect.

ALAN KNOTT

This chapter provides a comprehensive list of drills broken down into the following categories:

- Agility and fast feet
- Hand-eye co-ordination and reactions
- Catching the ball cleanly and giving with the ball
- Pre-match preparation
- Footwork
- Stood back and diving
- Stood up to seam and spin
- Run outs and other dismissals
- Training on your own

We list the equipment needed and describe how the drill works, with text and photos, additionally offering ideas for progression. We also hope that you will be inspired to adapt the drills specifically for your target audience, and even start producing your own drills.

Note for coaches

A powerful way of empowering a wicketkeeper to think for themselves is to place lots of coaching equipment on the floor and ask them to come up with their own practice drills. Remember, all players and coaches are different, and what works for one may not work for another. However, a wicketkeeper's overall aim should be executing the basics consistently over a long period of time. Players will very often do it their way, and if you are either a player or a coach, an honest assessment has to be made as to whether the skill is being performed on a consistent and safe basis. The answer to that question will lead you to the next step in the keeper's development.

Agility and fast feet

Ladder work

Equipment needed:
1 or 2 ladders (2–3 metres)
2–4 cones
Cricket balls or soft balls

Description:
Place the ladder as shown in the photo with the wicketkeeper(s) lined up at the end. At the other end place two cones where you will ask the wicketkeeper(s) to set in their ready position.

The first time through they traverse face on, placing both feet at pace in the gaps between the rungs of the ladder. Once out of the ladder, ask them to set in the ready position for a catch. They then jog back to the start of the ladder.

Second time through, they do this side on and then the third time its side on again, facing the opposite direction. Fourth and fifth time they can do one foot in, one foot out on one side and then work in the opposite direction.

Progression:

Add a second ladder off at right angles so they repeat before taking a second catch at the end.

Up the pace and difficulty of the footwork.

Throwing/hitting catches either side.

Catching in one hand only.

Ask wicketkeepers to rate their take after each catch.

The coach could impede the keeper's movement by the use of a resistance band placed around the keeper's waist. Resistance is to be applied from the appropriate angle.

Cone work 1

Equipment needed:

4 cones

1 cricket ball or soft ball

Description:

Set up four cones as overleaf with the wicketkeeper in the middle in the ready position. Give each cone a number. The coach calls out the number of the cone to move to with a chassé. The wicketkeeper moves back to the middle each time. Keep an eye out for them bobbing up and down. Repeat ten times for three sets with a 90-second rest between sets.

 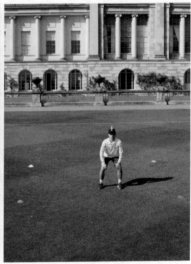

Progression:

Add a bean bag, cone or shuttlecock on top of the wicketkeeper's head so they have to keep head and eyes level.

Add a catch for the wicketkeeper to take after each repetition and ask them to rate it out of ten. As they get tired, can they keep the same quality of catch?

Add a catch to each rep. This time they have to chassé and place the ball on each cone. Once all cones are covered, they then chassé between the cones to collect each ball, return to the middle and then throw back to the coach.

Renumber the cones, so the keeper has to reorientate themselves.

The coach could impede the keeper's movement by the use of a resistance band placed around the keeper's waist. Resistance is to be applied from the appropriate angle.

Cone work 2

Equipment:
5 cones
5 cricket balls or soft balls

Description:
Set up the five cones and balls as shown. The wicketkeeper starts where the balls are, and one at a time places a ball on each cone. Second time through, the wicketkeeper collects the balls one at a time, returning them to their starting point. Repeat three times with a 90-second rest between sets.

Progression:

Hit/throw a catch to the keeper for each ball they have to place. When returning balls, the keeper can shy at a stump for each one from the starting position.

Time them and have a competition between the keepers doing the drill.

The coach could impede the keeper's movement by the use of a resistance band placed around the keeper's waist. Resistance is to be applied from the appropriate angle.

Cone work 3

Equipment:
8 cones

Description:
Place the cones in a straight line touching each other. Starting at the left cone, No. 1, place the left foot gently on the cone, with the right foot behind on the floor. Jump to the right, swapping feet so that the right foot is now gently on cone No. 2, left foot behind. Repeat, gently putting left foot on cone No. 3, right foot behind. Repeat to the end of the cones. The aim is to traverse the full length of the cones as quickly and as lightly as possible. Go back to cone No. 1 and repeat.

Progression:

Complete one length of eight cones, then jump and spin around in mid-air, to traverse down the other side of the cones. Continue repeating.

Reposition the cones to a random, scattered arrangement, and repeat the jump and swapping feet manoeuvre, traversing in forwards, backwards and sideways directions.

Crabbing race

Equipment:

2 cones

1 bean bag

Description:

Place two cones three metres apart. The wicketkeeper adopts a set position, halfway between the cones. They then crab sideways to their left, touch the cone, then crab all the way to their right and touch the other cone. Repeat.

Progression:

The coach records the time taken to complete four continuous lengths. Place a ball on one cone and reposition it after each length.

Have two keepers competing against each other by introducing another set of cones facing each other, thus setting up a direct race between the two.

Keepers balance a bean bag on their head.

The coach could impede the keeper's movement by the use of a resistance band placed around the keeper's waist. Resistance is to be applied from the appropriate angle.

Balloons

Equipment:
4 balloons

Description:
The wicketkeeper adopts a set position then has to keep one balloon in the air by tapping it up using either hand. The coach adds a second balloon, and the wicketkeeper now has to control both using either hand. The coach adds the third and fourth balloons.

Progression:

The coach records the time taken for being able to control two, three or four balloons.

Add more balloons. Attempt the drill using one hand only.

Swiss ball catches

Equipment:

1 Swiss ball

1 tennis ball

Description:

The wicketkeeper adopts the set position, two metres away from Swiss ball. The coach throws the tennis ball at the Swiss ball, which deflects at random angles. The keeper attempts to catch every deflection. The coach varies their start position. This is a great drill for replicating bat-pad catches.

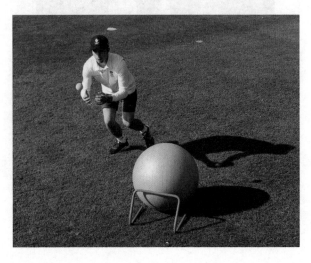

Progression:

The coach alters the angle and pace of their throw.

Use different coloured tennis balls and nominate right- or left-handed catches.

Hoops and hurdles

Equipment:

Hoops and hurdles

Description:

The coach lays out a group of hoops on the ground. The wicketkeeper randomly jumps into one, landing on both feet, keeping their balance, staying inside the cone. Repeat into the next hoop, then continue to repeat.

The coach lays out a symmetrical group of low hurdles. The keeper jumps over one hurdle and immediately jumps over another, landing on two feet. Continue to repeat, ensuring good balance.

Progression:

Hoop drill – the keeper lands on two feet and then adopts a one-legged Superman position, ensuring they do not overbalance and fall out of the hoop.

The keeper lands on one leg and adopts a one-legged Superman position.

Advance to catching a ball too.

The coach increases the distance between hoops.

Hurdles drill – the keeper lands on one foot only. Advance to catching a ball too.

Note for coaches

Although it is important to come to a session with a plan in mind depending on how advanced your wicketkeeper is, it is always important to ask a player what they want to work on and what areas of their game they feel are in good order and where they feel they could improve. This is not just your job – the player also needs to take ownership. They need opportunities to work things out for themselves, perhaps guided by some questioning. Some of the best sessions you can have are when you do not have to say much at all.

Hand-eye co-ordination and reactions

One-eyed catching

Equipment:
1 soft ball

Description:
Ask your wicketkeepers to stand a metre apart in their ready positions. Ask them to cover one eye with one hand. They then throw and catch with one eye and one hand for ten repetitions. Repeat throw, changing the eye and throwing hand. Repeat three times.

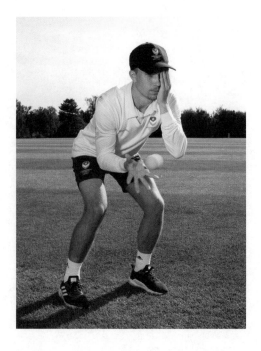

Progression:

Increase the distance between the wicketkeepers.

Time how many they can complete in a minute.

Back to zero – set the keepers a target to reach. If they drop one, they go back to zero until they complete the set number of repetitions.

Use cricket balls.

Multi-ball catching

Equipment:

2–5 soft balls

Description:

Ask your wicketkeepers to stand a metre apart. One will have both balls. A ball at a time is thrown from the right hand of one player to the left hand of the other player, who then does the same thing. Keep them going for a minute. If successful with two balls, move to three and keep adding to stretch them.

Progression:

Increase the distance between the wicketkeepers.

Competition – how many can they complete in a minute?

Back to zero – set the keepers a target to reach. If they drop one, they go back to zero until they complete the set number of repetitions.

Use a variety of different balls (shapes and sizes).

Ball drop

Equipment:

2 cricket balls

Description:

Ask your wicketkeepers to stand half a metre apart. One stands upright with both balls and arms extended out to the side. The other crouches low, facing the other.

The player with the balls releases one of them and the other has to take it before it hits the ground. The feeding player should just let the ball drop, not use a slight throwing action, as this gives the catcher a visual clue!

Progression:
Lower the arms of the feeding player.

Widen the arms of the feeding player.

Have the wicketkeepers taking the catches facing the other way.

Eye-focus string

Equipment:
5 metres of string
Markers set half a metre apart

Description:
The wicketkeepers have to stand facing each other holding the string at either end, pulled tight at eye level. The keepers focus their eyes on each marker one at a time working along the string and back again. They are not allowed to move on to the next marker until properly in focus. Repeat three times.

Progression:
Give each marker a number. The keepers take it in turns to call a number and the keeper has to focus on that marker. Repeat ten times.

Do with one eye closed and alternate eyes used.

Turn and catch

Equipment:
1 soft ball
2 cones

Description:
Set up two cones and ask your wicketkeeper to stand in the ready position facing away from you. On your call they turn quickly into a ready position facing you as you hit/throw a catch. Repeat ten times.

Progression:
Reduce the distance between the coach and wicketkeeper.
  Make the catch harder.
  Add some skyers.
  Make the keeper shy at a set of stumps after catching.

Katchet board work

Equipment:
1–4 Katchet boards
Cricket balls or light bowling machine balls
2 cones

Set up the Katchet boards and cones as shown, with the wicketkeeper in between the cones in a ready position. The board's ridges should face straight forward so the ball can deviate in either direction. Throw ten catches. Rest for 90 seconds and then repeat ten times.

Progression:

Move the boards closer to the wicketkeeper.

Add some stumps to mimic standing up to spinners.

Angle ridges so the take will be more to one side than the other.

Catch one-handed.

Underarm feed for really close work.

Reaction ball work

Equipment:

1 reaction ball

Description:

Have the wicketkeepers standing two metres apart in their ready positions as if stood up to spin bowling, throwing the ball underarm into the middle space between them. The reaction ball will deviate in direction. Aim for them to come up with the bounce of the ball.

Progression:
Throw the ball closer to each other.

Overarm throws to increase the pace of the throw.

Cone work

Equipment:
6 cones
Cricket balls

Description:
Place the cones randomly on a good length. Get the wicketkeeper to set up as though stood up to spin and stand two metres away but go down on one knee. Throw the cricket ball, aiming to land it in the cones to get deviations in multiple directions.

Progression:

Throw from closer/throw harder.

Add spin to your throw.

Move the cones fuller/shorter to vary length.

Add further debris, mats, etc.

Balloons

Equipment:

4 balloons

Description:

The wicketkeeper adopts the ready position. They have to keep one balloon up in the air by tapping it up using either hand. The coach adds a second balloon, so the keeper now has to control two balloons using either hand. The coach adds a third and fourth balloons.

Progression:

The coach records the time taken to be able to control two, three or four balloons.

Attempt the drill using one hand only.

Playing cards

Equipment:
Pack of playing cards

Description:
The wicketkeeper adopts a set position, approximately two metres from the coach. The coach holds a single playing card and throws it vertically into the air. The keeper attempts to catch it before it hits the ground.

Progression:
The coach holds two cards, one black and one red. They call a colour for the keeper to catch. The coach throws them together and the keeper has to identify the correct card and catch it before it hits the floor. Then progress to using two cards, both the same colour, but different numbers. Progress to three

cards, two with numbers on, the third being a royal. Call the royal, etc. Then have cards of the same colour, or different suits, etc. Keepers can compete against each other.

Swing-ball game

Equipment:
1 rubber swing-ball

Description:
The wicketkeeper adopts a set position, approximately ten metres from the coach. The coach throws the swing-ball underarm, at pace, straight towards the keeper, initiating either inswing or outswing to the ball. The keeper catches the ball one-handed, endeavouring to catch it in their right hand if the ball arrives on the right side of their body, or in their left hand if the ball arrives on the left side of their body.

Progression:

The coach alters their aim and the amount of swing to attempt to trick the keeper into catching the ball in the wrong hand; that is, the ball is caught in the left hand, but on the right side of the body. A competition between keeper and coach or between two keepers can be instigated.

Coloured tennis balls

Equipment:

2 different coloured tennis balls

Description:

The wicketkeeper adopts a set position, approximately four metres away from the coach. The coach throws both different coloured tennis balls underarm towards the keeper. As the coach throws, they call out which coloured ball the keeper should catch, two-handed. The other ball is ignored.

Progression:

The coach puts a single ball in each hand, hiding them behind their back. They then nominate a colour and simultaneously throw both balls underarm towards the wicketkeeper, who catches the nominated ball.

Further progression can take the form of 'not' catching the nominated colour, but the other one. The keeper starts with their back to the coach, turning around as the coach calls the colour. Progress on to diving catches and a bounced throw.

Catching clock

Description:

The wicketkeeper adopts a set position. The coach calls out an hourly time from one o'clock to 12 o'clock. The keeper quickly

moves their hands and body into the correct position for the time called.

Progression:

The keeper scores points for the correct positioning of hands, head, feet, hips, etc.

A competition can be set up between keepers.

Introduce a ball for realism.

Roll a foam dice to determine catching clock glove position.

Equipment:
Boxing gloves
Boxing pads

Description:
The wicketkeeper wears the boxing gloves and the coach wears the boxing pads. The keeper punches the coach's pads in a planned routine.

Progression:
The coach constantly moves the pads around and keeps amending the hitting sequence previously agreed with the keeper.

Katchet board under sight screen

Equipment:
Sight screen
Katchet board
10 cricket balls

Description:
The Katchet board is located centrally under the sight screen. The coach is positioned to one side of the screen, the wicketkeeper is on the other, positioned a suitable distance away from the board. The coach throws the ball on to the board and the keeper is suddenly presented with a catch out of nowhere, either straight or diving. The keeper resets and shouts, 'Ready,' then the coach throws another ball.

Progression:
Introduce a scoring system to encourage competition.

Add another board next to the other to manipulate more diving catches.

Reposition the keeper or offset the boards to encourage more left- or right-handed catches.

Hidden wall catch

Equipment:
Set of stumps
1 tennis ball

Description:

The wicketkeeper is set up approximately four metres back from a wall, next to the stumps, as though standing up to the wicket. The coach is a further two metres behind the keeper, set up slightly to their off side. The keeper is facing directly towards the wall or rebound catching net, with their back to the coach. The coach throws the ball at pace on to the wall, ensuring that the ball bounces before it reaches the keeper. Repeat numerous times.

Progression:

The coach throws the ball at different positions on the wall, ensuring that the keeper has numerous positions to take the ball in, i.e., off side or leg side, short or full.

The coach can also reposition themself down the leg side of the keeper to change the angle.

The keeper can also reorientate themself to set up for a left-handed batter.

A form of competition can be introduced. One point for the keeper for every clean take. One point for the coach if there is a fumble. A bonus point can be awarded for something brilliant.

Different types of ball could be introduced for extra pace and bounce.

Pads strapped together and placed in front of the stumps could replicate a batter, giving both deflections and a visual obstruction for leg-side takes.

Description:

A very good way of training your eyes is to watch birds or insects in flight, particularly during the summer months. Swallows, swifts and house martins always fly very quickly in random directions, so pick one and keep your eyes fully focused on it, no matter how far away or close it is to you. Do the same for insects and butterflies. There are also many eye reaction-time games to be found on the internet that will enhance your vision and reactions.

Catching the ball cleanly and giving with the ball

To aid catching and giving with the ball, work with lighter balls. As well as incrediballs you can get some good lighter bowling machine balls that work well. The ultimate test of whether a ball is caught cleanly is to use a tennis ball hit at pace. Only if the timing of the take and the give are good will the ball stay in.

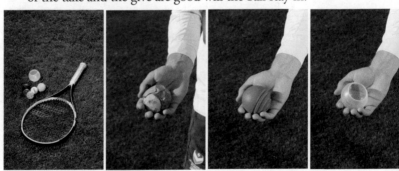

A great drill is to get the keeper standing up to the stumps, and with a tennis racket serve the tennis ball overarm, replicating the bowler bowling. Vary the pitching line and length and increase/decrease the pace to suit.

Note for coaches

Remember to ask the wicketkeeper to rate their take out of ten for each, whether with a lighter ball or a cricket ball.

Pre-match preparation

Covering the basics

Equipment:
1 cricket ball

Description:
Stand two metres from the wicketkeeper and hit/throw the following catches:

10 x low catches
10 x waist-high catches
10 x shoulder-height and above
10 x either side of the body
10 x one-handed catches – both hands
10 x diving both sides (one- and two-handed)

Dog-stick warm-up

Equipment:
Dog-stick
Cricket ball

Description:
This drill is appropriate for wicketkeepers stood back or up to the wicket and replicates a bowler bowling the ball. The keeper adopts a set position appropriate for the speed of the delivery, and the coach uses the dog-stick to deliver the ball.

Progression:

The coach varies the speed, line and length delivered to the keeper.

Use a variety of balls, both new and old, colour appropriate for the game ahead.

Feed the ball either seam up or scrambled so that the keeper can identify it, encouraging them to watch the ball closely.

A cricket ball with adhesive sticky tape placed around one side is a great way to practise taking the swinging ball.

Stood up practice

Equipment:
Cricket ball
Light bowling machine ball
Flexi-stump

Description:
Ideally, your wicketkeeper will be able to do some keeping to the bowlers, but they may also like some shadow work. A simple way of doing this is to set up a flexi-stump on a wicket end, or even outfield, and throw balls of various lengths so that they bounce once. You are targeting the stump to try to get small deflections from it.

Note for coaches

It is important that during your pre-match preparation, all drills use the specific colour ball you will be playing with in the match.

Progression:

Throw harder/from closer.

Throw fuller.

Add some spin to your throw.

Use two flexi-stumps next to each other, but with a gap between them.

A cricket ball with adhesive sticky tape placed around one side is a great way to practise taking the swinging ball.

The coach could impede the keeper's movement by the use of a resistance band placed around the keeper's waist. Resistance is to be applied from the appropriate angle.

Note for coaches

A great drill is to get the keeper standing up to the stumps, and with a tennis racket serve the tennis ball overarm, replicating the bowler bowling. Vary the pitching line and length and increase/decrease the pace to suit.

Footwork

Side-to-side chassé and catch

Equipment:

2–4 cones

1 or 2 cricket balls

Description:

Set two cones three metres apart and place the wicketkeeper in the middle. Ask them to set up in the ready position as if stood back from the wicket. Hit the keeper a catch straight at them. The keeper takes the catch (with preferred method) then returns the ball and chassés across to one of the cones and back to the middle again before taking another catch. Repeat ten times. Do three sets with a 90-second rest between each.

Progression:
Have multiple balls and ask the keeper to have an underarm shy at a set of stumps after completing each catch. Place a bean bag, cone or shuttlecock on the keeper's head.

Throw a diving catch in the opposite direction to the cone they have to chassé to. The keeper then has to get up before chasséing. This is tiring and also good to work fitness.

If you have three wicketkeepers, make a rectangle with four cones. One keeper works for ten catches, chasséing between cones. The other keepers throw a catch when the keeper reaches their cone.

The coach could impede the keeper's movement by the use of a resistance band placed around the keeper's waist. Resistance is to be applied from the appropriate angle.

Cone work 1

Equipment needed:
4 cones
1 cricket ball or soft ball

Description:
Set up four cones as below with the wicketkeeper in the middle in the ready position. Give each cone a number. The coach calls out the number of the cone to move to with a chassé. The wicketkeeper moves back to the middle each time. Keep an eye out for bobbing up and down. Repeat ten times for three sets with a 90-second rest between sets.

Progression:

Add a catch for the wicketkeeper to take after each repetition and ask them to rate it out of ten. As they get tired, can they keep the same quality of catch?

Add a catch to each rep. This time they have to chassé and place the ball on each cone. Once all cones are covered, they then chassé between the cones to collect each ball, return to the middle and then throw back to the coach.

The coach could impede the keeper's movement by the use of a resistance band placed around the keeper's waist. Resistance is to be applied from the appropriate angle.

Note for coaches

This drill could be introduced into a group fielding session, set up around the keeper's stumps, when they are catching balls thrown back after fielders have taken skyed catches.

Stood back and diving

Standing back, my favourite drill is still to throw underarm catches to the wicketkeeper, either straight at him or occasionally to the right as though it's an edge. Very simple, though an effective way to stretch a keeper and increase pace as he or she improves.

PETER MOORES

You will need to hit or throw hundreds of catches to work on technique. When working on diving catch technique, an underarm feed is recommended for accuracy of height and distance. Remember to progress to throwing some straight, with just a few to dive for to test concentration. Hold some back to check for balance and any detrimental premeditating movement. Finally progress to random throws, straight, to each side, or diving each side. For indoor training, judo mats or crash mats can be used.

Note for coaches

The quality of your feed to the wicketkeeper is as important as the advice you give them, whether throwing, dog-sticking, hitting or on a machine. When drilling technique, the consistency and pace of the feed is important, just like it is when giving a batter throw-downs. When on a bowling machine, you would not drill a cover drive at 85mph initially. You would work at a lower speed at first to master the technique before adding pace to ramp up the difficulty and the realism.

Goalkeeping

My favourite drill as a player was the coach, Bob Carter, just hitting balls, with pace, accurately and realistically, using a goal I had to defend.
DAVID RIPLEY

Equipment:
2 cones or stumps
Cricket balls

Description:
Set up two cones to make a goal at a distance you think your wicketkeeper can cover. The coach stands a few metres away and hits/throws the ball, attempting to score a goal. The keeper is trying to catch all balls to prevent a goal. Complete ten and keep score. Do three sets with a 90-second rest between sets. Make sure the wicketkeeper sets up in the ready position before each catch, ensuring a good posture position.

Progression:

Make the goal bigger.

First to ten competition. The coach gets a point for each goal and dropped catch. The keeper gets a point for each catch or for a save if the ball does not carry.

One-handed catches only.

A cricket ball with adhesive sticky tape placed around one side is a great way to practise taking the swinging ball.

Note for coaches

Remember to hit some catches that do not carry so the wicketkeeper can work on this skill as well.

Kneeling dives for two-handed catches

Equipment:

Cricket ball

Description:

The wicketkeeper adopts a kneeling position, facing the coach. The coach, five metres away, throws an underarm catch to the keeper, either side of their body, wide enough for them to initiate a dive.

Progression:

Develop a scoring system, whereby the good technique elements are rewarded.

A cricket ball with adhesive sticky tape placed around one side is a great way to practise taking the swinging ball.

Deflection mat work

Shower mats, turned upside down, provide amazing results for stood-back work. Companies that provide public swimming pool equipment can supply these. They can be angled so that you can focus on a specific side. You will still get a few that go straight through to the keeper, and occasionally the opposite direction. It is great practice, as the keeper must concentrate, be patient and then explode to take a great diving catch.

You can feed on to these mats using a bowling machine. The outcome is better than using a Katchet board with a bowling machine because you get a lower bounce, therefore more realistic in terms of catching height. You can also manually throw on to them with cricket balls, and the lighter bowling machine balls also work well. You can also add some slip fielders in, as there will be some big deflections. This enables the keeper and first slip to practise together, helping with their set-up position orientation and their catch decision-making reactions.

If outside, you can even get bowlers bowling on to them. This provides great target bowling work for them and high-quality realistic training for the wicketkeepers. Slips could again be added for realistic practice.

Katchet boards and fielding machine

Katchet boards also work well for manually thrown catches and these can be angled to work specific sides. They do not work as realistically with a normal high bowling machine but work well with a lower positioned fielding machine on its legs.

Note for coaches

If you are fortunate to have one of these machines at your disposal, why not set up pre-match for your wicketkeeper to practise on?

You can also hold an angled bat in front of a fielding machine to deliver deflections (wear batting gloves for safety). This also works well with the Katchet board.

Bowling machine work

As well as using a bowling machine firing balls on to deflection mats, it is also a good tool to practise keeping to a swinging ball, as you can input large amounts of swing, thus mimicking the movement of the ball after it has beaten the batter. Additionally, if you set a normal machine to zero swing, you can mimic a wobbling ball reasonably well, as the ball does not actually go completely straight but can move slightly in different directions.

You can also add a shadow batter to this practice, batting with some foam pipe lagging. The batter will nick a few and give the keeper some realistic edge practice.

Note for coaches

Remember, on all bowling machine work it is always useful to do some 'dummy' feeds to check the keeper's balance/set-up position prior to release of the ball. A 'dummy' feed is where you initiate the ball feed process, but do not let the ball drop into the machine.

This is very realistic practice, and you get some great deflections.

Dog-stick diving catches

Equipment:
Dog-stick
Cricket ball
Stumps
Katchet boards
Shower mats

Description:
This drill is appropriate for wicketkeepers stood back and replicates a fast bowler hitting the outside or inside edge of the batter's bat. The keeper adopts a set position, set back from the

stumps, a distance appropriate for the speed of the delivery. Katchet boards or upturned shower mats are positioned around a good length and the coach uses the dog-stick to deliver the ball, looking to hit the deflection equipment as often as possible.

Progression:
The coach varies the speed, line and length delivered to the keeper.

Competition introduced, i.e., the wicketkeeper has to take five catches. If dropped, they go back to zero.

If the coach reduces the pace or delivers a soft machine ball, the keeper could possibly stand up to the stumps.

A cricket ball with adhesive sticky tape placed around one side is a great way to practise taking the swinging ball.

Stood back, my favourite drill is with a bowling machine on the floor and a bat in front of the machine. It is set on 65mph. The coach misses some deliberately and then hits some to get a nick effect. It really stretches me to the max and is very realistic practice. I get that feeling the nick is very similar to a match and comes fast so my reactions need to be sharp.

TOM MOORES

Bat skim catches

Equipment:
Cricket ball
Stumps
Cricket bat or fielding bat

Description:
This drill is appropriate for wicketkeepers stood back, and replicates a fast bowler hitting the outside or inside edge of the batter's bat. The keeper adopts a set position, set back from the stumps, a distance appropriate for the speed of the delivery. The coach holds the bat outstretched horizontally in their non-throwing hand, aiming it towards the keeper. They then throw the ball on to the bat face, skimming it off the surface, the angle of deflection being determined by the angle the bat is held at. This can also be done with a bowling machine on the floor.

Progression:

The coach varies the angle and direction of deflection.

Competition introduced, i.e., the keeper has to take five catches. If they drop one, they go back to zero.

The distance between the coach and keeper could be reduced.

The angle of deflection is increased.

The ball is deflected into the ground before it reaches the keeper.

The ball is fed through a bowling machine onto a bat.

Wobbling ball

To work on taking a wobbling ball you will need a brand new ball. The art for the coach is to try to hit the ball seam up to the wicketkeeper. This might be easier with a cricket bat and by driving the ball. Some coins securely taped to a ball also provide a good way of creating a wobbling ball, as does an old plastic washing machine liquid dispensing ball when hit off a tennis racket. Custom manufactured balls, swing-balls and weighted balls, for example, can also be used.

Slip-catching practice

It is always advantageous to get the wicketkeeper involved in the slip-catching practice, as it is very realistic because they will not get a chance every ball, thus exercising their powers of concentration. It also gives them a chance to practise setting the slip cordon up correctly.

Stood up to the wicket for seam and spin

Shadow batting

*Standing up, I still think shadow batting
is great practice for any wicketkeeper.*
PETER MOORES

The best practice for standing up to the wicket is to have a shadow batter. It is important that the batter kits up for realism, using their own bat, as you want them to bat as realistically as they would in a game, whilst ensuring they miss the ball. You can also ask them to play a range of shots.

Batting with some foam pipe lagging is a great way to get realistic edges for the wicketkeeper to take. A coach can throw these or safely use any type of bowling machine. A normal height machine is ideal for standing up to seam, as is a lower height fielding machine, as this replicates lower bounce as well. You can subtly alter line and length and the amount of swing on a normal machine to enable match realism.

There is some good footage here of a shadow batting session: https://youtu.be/tSOK519usx4

If you do not have a player to shadow bat, then place an object such as an upturned kit bag, box, tall cones or football mannequin to replicate a batter. Hang a towel or jacket over them to obscure the view more.

Note for coaches

Remember, on all bowling machine work it is always useful to do some 'dummy' feeds to check the keeper's balance/set-up position prior to release of the ball. A 'dummy' feed is where you initiate the ball feed process, but do not let the ball drop into the machine.

Of course, if you do not have a machine it is fine to throw these takes. You can use new balls and get them swinging and remember to frequently hold back and initiate a dummy feed on some of your releases, to check balance on set-up. You can also throw spin as well. A cricket ball with adhesive sticky tape placed around one side is a great way to practise taking the swinging ball.

Additionally, get your bowlers bowling to the keeper with a shadow batter. You can outline targets for the bowlers to hit so they are working on their skills, and even ask the batter to play normally with a bat but miss the occasional ball. This builds concentration, as the keeper will only take a few balls and will not know when they are coming through to them.

If you have access to a Merlyn machine, this enables brilliant practice for standing up to spin. Variations can be made to the amounts of turn, line and length, and the pace of each ball. You can also let it self-feed while you shadow bat. A Merlyn machine also has several different 'variation' settings to keep the wicketkeeper guessing as to what type of delivery they are about to receive.

There are also many other objects you can use apart from foam pipe lagging to simulate edges. You can use a standard cone, a folded bowler's target mat, a flexi-stump or a piece of cardboard. Some coaches even make up their own snick bat.

Remember, putting a thin wooden board down on the surface provides a lower bounce; therefore, you can work on taking the lower balls, checking whether the keeper is coming up with the bounce of the ball.

Leg-side work

Any bowling machine is good to use for leg-side work, but predominantly all you will have is coach and keeper, a set of stumps and some balls. Initially, from a kneeling position, you can simply underarm some full toss takes, positioning yourself where the ball would be pitching. The keeper should stay in their stance until they need to move leg side. After drilling the method leg side, also throw some straight to check they are not moving too early, working on concentration, balance and a good posture.

Progress on to throwing the ball from the bowling crease, landing the ball on various lengths down the leg side, continually checking via dummy feeds that the keeper is not moving too early, anticipating the leg-side delivery. A cricket ball with adhesive sticky tape placed around one side is a great way to practise taking the swinging ball. The coach could impede the keeper's movement by the use of a resistance band placed around the keeper's waist. Resistance is to be applied from the appropriate angle.

Rough

To practise taking the ball from the rough, replicating unusual
deviations, you can use any debris, such as screwed-up newspaper,
target mats, batting gloves, cones, etc., positioned on the pitch.
Delivery of the ball can be by throwing, bowling or bowling
machine.

Inner glove and cone nicks

Equipment:
Inner glove
Batting glove
Cone
Cricket ball
Stumps

Description:
The wicketkeeper sets up in position next to the stumps. The coach is approximately four metres away. Another player acts as the batter, wearing their right-hand batting glove for safety purposes, and gently dangles a wicketkeeping inner glove from it. The coach underarm feeds a full toss through to the

keeper. As the ball reaches the batter, they attempt to nick the ball on its way through to the keeper. The keeper takes the catch. The ball is returned to the coach. Repeat.

Progression:
The batter replaces the inner glove with a plastic cone and continues to nick the ball as it goes through to the keeper.

The speed and height of the throw can be increased, or the throwing distance shortened.

The batter can shout abruptly to distract the keeper.

Reorientate the batter to act as a left-hander and repeat the drill. Increase the pace and realism by throwing overarm, bounced throws.

Run-around keeping drill

Equipment:
Cricket ball
Stumps

Description:
Two wicketkeepers and a coach are required for this drill. One keeper sets up at the stumps, as if stood up to the wicket. The other stands in the batter's position, also facing the coach, who is standing approximately four metres away. The coach feeds an underarm full toss through to the keeper; the batting keeper lets it pass through. The keeper returns the ball to the coach. The keepers quickly swap position in a clockwise direction, staying in

a front-on position. The keeper now becomes the batter and vice versa. After an initial familiarisation period, the batting keeper can occasionally catch the ball, thus preventing it going through to the keeper. Keep rotating and repeating as quickly as possible.

Progression:
Progress to leg-side takes, ensuring the batter catches some occasionally. The batter can fake a catch, pretending to catch, and then open their hands at the last second. Also set up for a left-handed batter. Introduce some form of point-scoring competition.

Stump distraction game

Equipment:
Cricket ball
2 flexi-stumps
Stumps

Description:
Two wicketkeepers and a coach are required for this drill. One

keeper sets up at the stumps, as if stood up to the wicket. The other stands in the batter's position holding a flexi-stump in each hand. The coach is standing approximately four metres away. The coach feeds an underarm full toss at pace through to the keeper. The batting keeper raises and lowers both hands in a crossing motion as the ball passes. The keeper attempts to either take the ball off the edge of one of the flexi-stumps or complete a clean take should the ball miss both flexi-stumps. The keepers take it in turns.

Progression:

Introduce some form of point-scoring competition.

The batter can shout abruptly to distract the keeper.

Reorientate the batter to act as a left-hander and repeat the drill.

Use overarm, bounced throws. The keeper can initiate a stumping.

Run outs and other dismissals

Either end shy

Equipment:
10 cricket balls
2 flexi-stumps

Description:
Set up a wicket, ideally on an actual wicket, with the two flexi-stumps. The coach stands where the batter would be and the wicketkeeper is behind the flexi-stump in the stood-up set-up position. The coach rolls the ball out either side (varying angles) and nominates an end where the keeper must shy for a run out. Keep score out of ten for direct hits.

Progression:

Add some fielders to back up the keeper's throw, who then have to return the ball to the coach. The coach now nominates whether the keeper should go for a direct hit or over the top of the stumps to the fielder. Depending on the call, the fielders either come in and take the ball from the keeper or they back up the throw.

Vary with some top-edged sweep catches for the wicketkeeper to take as well. They can still then go for a shy.

Add a pair of batters running between the wickets.

Catch and shy

Equipment:
Set of stumps or flexi-stump
10 cricket balls

Description:

This drill is ideally done from a wicket facing towards the boundary but can also be set up on the outfield. Located beside the stumps or flexi-stump, the coach hits a catch to the wicketkeeper, who should be standing where they would normally stand back to a fast bowler. After taking the catch, the keeper must shy at the stumps. They score one point for taking the catch and one point for a direct hit. Using ten balls, how many do they score out of 20?

Progression:

Offer bonus points for double play and double points for something brilliant.

Keeper vs coach competition: the coach gets a point for each catch dropped and stumps missed; the keeper gets a point for a catch and direct hit.

Hit some balls that do not carry to increase the level of difficulty.

Promote the keeper to perform some diving takes. Can they bounce up to one knee to get the shy away quickly?

Add a skyer occasionally. Once caught, get the keeper to take off their glove and throw in over the top of the stumps.

Sliding retrieve

Equipment:
Cricket balls
2 sets of stumps

Description:
The coach rolls out a ball so that wherever it is the wicketkeeper has to chase it down. The distances and speed should replicate those experienced in a match situation. They then execute a sliding retrieve and jump up to shy at the stumps.

Progression:
Introduce some form of point-scoring competition.

The coach nominates which set of stumps the keeper is to throw at.

The coach rolls out balls, one after the other, randomly at different angles. The keeper chases each one down, throws and gets physically overloaded.

Note for coaches

If this drill is done outside it may be necessary to water the ground locally to the practice area, or if indoors it may be beneficial to sprinkle talcum powder on the crash mats used.

Taking stumps run out

Equipment:
Crazy Catch net
Cricket balls

Description:
The wicketkeeper sets up in front of the stumps.

The coach throws a ball into the Crazy Catch and rebounds it towards the keeper, who takes the ball and gives towards the stumps to effect a run out.

Progression:
Vary the angles of the throw to replicate the ball coming in from different parts of the outfield.

After taking the bails off at one end, the keeper goes for a direct hit at the bowler's end. Can the keeper achieve a 'double play'?

Training on your own

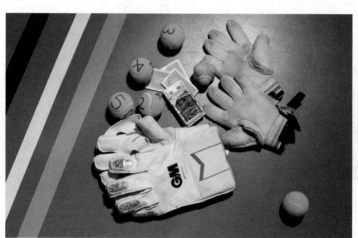

Rebound takes off a wall

Equipment:
Set of stumps
Tennis ball

Batting pads
Kit bag

Description:
The wicketkeeper is set up approximately four metres back from a wall, next to the stumps, as though stood up to the wicket, facing directly towards the wall. The keeper throws the ball at pace, on to the wall, ensuring that the rebound bounces before it returns to them. Repeat several times, ensuring that the ball rebounds on both off side and leg side. Wicketkeeping gloves are not required, but the keeper may want to wear their keeping inners.

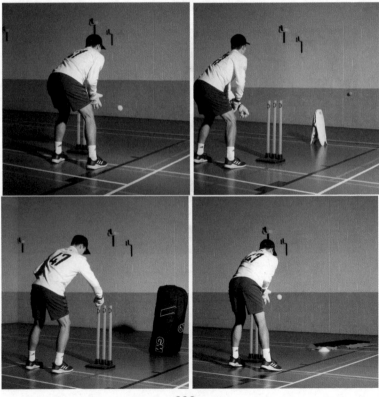

Progression:

The keeper throws the ball at different positions on to the wall, ensuring that they manoeuvre to take the ball correctly, i.e., off side or leg side, short or full.

The keeper can also reorientate to set up for a left-handed batter.

A form of competition can be introduced to reward clean takes, good bases, etc.

Different types and sizes of ball could be introduced for extra pace and bounce.

Pads strapped together and placed in front of the stumps could replicate a batter, giving both deflections and a visual obstruction for leg-side takes.

Introduce stumpings after every take.

A large kit bag, placed vertically on the location where the batter would be is great for practising leg-side takes where sight of the ball is lost momentarily.

Introduce debris on to the ball landing area for extra turn and bounce, e.g., cones, mats, clothing, etc.

Diving rebound catches off a wall

Equipment:
Tennis ball
Katchet board
Shower mats
Crash mat

Description:

The wicketkeeper is set up approximately four metres back from a wall, facing directly towards the wall. The board or mat is located approximately two metres from the wall or keeper. The keeper throws the ball at pace on to the board or mat and catches the deflected ball rebounding off the wall. Repeat several times. Wicketkeeping gloves are not required, but the keeper may want to wear their keeping inners.

Progression:

The keeper can also realign themself offset to the board or mat, so that they can control the width of the right- or left-handed dives.

A form of competition can be introduced to reward catches.

Different types and sizes of ball could be introduced for extra pace and bounce.

A crash mat is recommended to dive when this drill is done indoors.

Wall corner catching

Equipment:
Tennis ball

Description:
The wicketkeeper is set up approximately one metre back from the corner of a wall, facing directly towards it. The keeper underarm throws the ball at pace on to the wall, ensuring that the rebound bounces across the corner, hitting the opposite wall, before it returns to them. The ball is caught two-handed. Repeat several times. The keeper should be set in a comfortable position, keeping their feet totally still. Wicketkeeping gloves are not required, but the keeper may want to wear their keeping inners.

Progression:

The keeper throws the ball at different positions on to the wall, ensuring they execute clean takes.

A form of competition can be introduced to reward clean catches.

A timed game could be introduced to record how long it takes to do 20 catches.

Different types and sizes of ball could be introduced for extra pace, etc.

One-handed catch only.

Overarm throws could be introduced, in association with the ball rebounding on to the floor just before the take, so distance from the keeper to wall corner is amended accordingly.

Swiss ball bat-and-pad catches

Equipment:
Tennis ball
Swiss ball

Description:

The wicketkeeper is set up approximately four metres back from a wall, facing directly towards it. A Swiss ball is placed two metres from the wall and supported to stop it moving. The tennis ball is thrown on to the wall at pace, so that it returns without bouncing to directly hit the Swiss ball. The position the tennis ball hits the Swiss ball will determine the height, angle and trajectory of the catch. It could be an edged catch, or a forward bat-and-pad catch. Repeat several times. Wicketkeeping gloves are not required, but the keeper may want to wear their keeping inners. The Swiss ball could be repositioned against the wall, and the keeper throws directly at it, then manoeuvres to take the corresponding catch.

Progression:
Use different size balls.

Create a scoring competition.

Use different coloured tennis balls to differentiate two- or one-handed catches.

Nominate two- or one-handed catches depending on where the catch is taken.

Wall tennis

Equipment:
Tennis ball

Description:
The wicketkeeper is set up approximately one metre back from a wall, facing directly towards it. The keeper taps the ball against the wall using their fingers and palms of their hands, alternating left hand, right hand, keeping the ball from dropping to the floor. Repeat several times. The keeper should be set in a comfortable position, keeping their feet totally still. Wicketkeeping gloves are not required, but the keeper may want to wear their keeping inners.

Progression:

The keeper hits the ball at different heights or positions on the wall, ensuring they keep the ball from hitting the floor.

A form of competition can be introduced.

The keeper moves nearer to the wall whilst the drill is in progress, or moves further away, whilst keeping the ball active.

A timed game could be introduced to record how long it takes to do 20 catches.

Different types and sizes of ball could be introduced for extra pace, etc.

The keeper could progress to three consecutive left-hand hits before swapping to three consecutive right-hand hits.

Reverse hand rebounds

Equipment:
Tennis ball

Description:
The wicketkeeper is set up approximately one metre back from a wall, facing directly towards it. The keeper gently underarm throws the ball against the wall. Upon its return, if the ball is slightly on the left side of their body, they catch it in their right hand, ensuring that the hand has reversed, i.e., the little finger is higher than the thumb, which is now pointing at the ground. Repeat several times for both right- and left-handed takes. The keeper should be set in a comfortable position, keeping their feet totally still. Wicketkeeping gloves are not required, but the

keeper may want to wear their keeping inners. This is a great drill for developing wrist flexibility, essential for producing large catching areas for two-handed, high-side takes.

Progression:
A form of competition can be introduced, rewarding points for good technique.

Numbered tennis balls

Equipment:
12 numbered tennis balls

Description:
The wicketkeeper is set up approximately four metres back from a wall, facing directly towards it. Behind them is a collection of 12 tennis balls randomly lying on the floor. Each tennis ball has a large number written on it four times in felt-tip pen, equally spaced around the ball. Balls are numbered 1–6, and there should be two of each number. Without looking at the ball, the keeper picks one up and overarm throws it against the wall at pace, ensuring it bounces once. After catching the ball, the keeper calls out the number seen written on it as it was moving. This is a great drill for enhancing watching the ball.

Progression:
A form of competition can be introduced, rewarding correct identification of the numbered ball.

Balls are thrown from a position nearer to the wall.

Line and length are altered to increase the difficulty in identification, i.e., leg-side, yorker, good length, short.

Two balls at once

Equipment:
2 tennis balls

Description:
The wicketkeeper is set up approximately half a metre back from a wall, facing directly towards it. With a ball in each hand, the keeper gently underarm throws them against the wall, and after rebounding, catches both balls, one in each hand. The height of each ball is to remain the same.

Progression:
A form of competition can be introduced, rewarding catching a certain number of balls consecutively.

The keeper could move further away from the wall incrementally to approximately two metres or more.

The height of each ball can be varied, or even crossed over in flight!

Crazy Net catching

Equipment:
Crazy Net
A variety of different sizes and makes of ball

Description:
The wicketkeeper is set up approximately two metres back from a wall, facing directly towards the Crazy Net that is resting

against it. The keeper underarm throws the ball on to the net, taking a two-handed return catch. Repeat several times.

Progression:
A form of competition can be introduced, rewarding catching a certain number of balls consecutively or within a certain timeframe.

Move further away from the net incrementally to approximately four metres or more.

Overarm throws generating more pace could be introduced. All catches to be taken one-handed only.

Angle of net realigned to promote half-volley takes, etc.

Flexi-stumps could be added in front of the keeper for added deflections.

Balloons

Equipment:
4 balloons

Description:
The wicketkeeper adopts a set position. They have to keep one balloon up in the air by tapping it up using either hand. They add a second balloon and have to control two balloons using either hand. They subsequently add the third and fourth balloons.

Progression:
Record time for being able to control two, three

or four balloons before one of them hits the floor.

Attempt the drill using one hand only.

Half-volley takes

Equipment:
Set of stumps
Variety of different size/soft balls

Description:
The wicketkeeper is set up approximately four metres back from a wall, next to the stumps, as though stood up to the wicket, facing directly towards the wall. The keeper throws the ball at pace on to the wall, ensuring that the rebound bounces

on a half-volley or very full length. Repeat several times, ensuring that the ball rebounds on both off side and leg side. Wicketkeeping gloves are not required, but the keeper may want to wear their keeping inners. The keeper is to ensure that they stay low, catch two-handed and watch the ball without flinching their head away.

Progression:

The keeper throws the ball at different positions on to the wall, ensuring that they manoeuvre to take the ball correctly, i.e., off side or leg side.

The keeper can also reorientate to set up for a left-handed batter.

A form of competition can be introduced to reward clean takes, staying low, not flinching, etc.

Different types of ball could be introduced for extra pace and bounce.

Complete a stumping or run out after each take.

Run out throwing

Equipment:
Set of tennis balls
Set of cricket balls
Stumps
Fielding net

Description:
A set of stumps is placed in front of a fielding net approximately ten metres away from the wicketkeeper. The keeper overarm throws the balls at the stumps, trying to effect a run out. This can be done from a standing, kneeling or sitting position, replicating potential match scenarios. The keeper should also throw with an underarm technique. Repeat several times. Wicketkeeping gloves are not required, but the keeper may want to wear their keeping inners.

Progression:

Create a scoring or timed competition.

Increase the throwing distance to replicate throwing to the non-striker's end.

Wear keeping gloves, removing one to throw.

Throw a rebound catch off a wall before throwing.

Complete a dive then attain a sitting, kneeling or standing position to execute the throw.

Equipment:
Tennis ball
Tennis racket

Description:
The wicketkeeper stands approximately five metres away from a wall, facing directly towards it. The ball is hit firmly towards the wall with the racket, aimed so that it is then caught in the weaker hand. Repeat several times. Wicketkeeping gloves are not required, but the keeper may want to wear their keeping inners.

Progression:
Create a scoring or timed competition.

Decrease the hitting distance. Increase the power of the hit.

Use a squash ball or golf ball.

Ball bounces on the floor prior to being caught.

Cone nicks

Equipment:
Plastic cone
Tennis ball

Description:
The wicketkeeper holds a plastic cone in their left hand and underarm throws the ball on to the wall. Upon its return, they nick the ball with the cone and take the catch in their right hand. This is repeated with the right hand holding the cone and the left hand throwing and catching the ball. The catching hand can be placed close to the nicking cone.

Progression:
Throw the ball overarm, increasing the pace of the throw.

Place the catching hand further away from the cone to take wider nicks.

Ensure that the ball bounces off the floor before taking the catch.

Equipment:
1 reaction ball

Description:
The wicketkeeper stands approximately two metres away from a wall, in a strong set position, then throws the reaction ball on to it, with an underarm throw, ensuring the reaction ball lands in front of them. The ball will deviate both laterally and vertically. The keeper looks to catch the ball cleanly in two hands.

Progression:
Let the ball bounce twice with a softer throw.

Throw the ball overarm, with increased pace and different pitching lengths.

Add a set of stumps to practise stumpings.

Playing cards

Equipment:
Pack of playing cards

Description:
The wicketkeeper adopts a set position, holding a single playing card. The card is then firmly thrown vertically into the air. They attempt to catch it before it hits the ground.

Progression:
The keeper holds two cards, one black and one red. They select a colour to catch. The cards are firmly thrown together and the keeper has to identify the correct card and catch it before it hits

the floor. Then progress to using two cards, both the same colour, but different numbers. Progress to three cards, two with numbers on, the third being a royal. Call the royal, etc. Then have cards of the same colour, or different suits, etc.

ABOUT THE AUTHORS

JAMES KNOTT

Having come through the junior ranks at Kent, James played professional cricket for MCC Young Cricketers, Surrey and Somerset for eight years between 1994 and 2001, making 24 appearances for Surrey's 1st XI. Following on from that he played nine years of minor counties cricket for Bedfordshire, captaining for three of those. He made several appearances for the representative Minor Counties XI and also the ECB XI (England amateurs) that won the European Championship in 2004.

As a coach, James has been the Head of Cricket at Stowe School since 2004, finishing top of the national school's cricket league twice, winning the Schools Arch Trophy twice and twice made it to the semi-finals of the National T20. Several pupils have gone on to play professional cricket in that time – Mark Nelson (Northants), Graeme White (Northants, Notts & England Lions), Ben Howgego (Northants), Liam Gough (MCC YC's and Essex), with the most high-profile being Ben Duckett (Northants, Notts & England Test, ODI & T20). Several others have gone on to MCCU (Marylebone Cricket Club Universities) programmes at

Loughborough, Cambridge, Oxford and Durham, as well as to play minor counties cricket. Current pupil at the school, James Cronie, is on the Northants academy and represented the Midlands at the Bunbury Festival and the Super 4s, and is currently training with the England U-19 squad.

As a writer, James has had several cricket articles published and one fictional short story.

ANDY O'CONNOR

Andy came through the junior system at Northants, playing for both the academy and 2nd XI. The remainder of his 25-year playing career consisted of playing in the Birmingham League, and predominantly the Northamptonshire Premier League, also representing the county in the Northants Amateur League XI.

Whilst playing local league cricket, Andy pursued a 25-year career in civil engineering, working as a design engineer for civil engineering consultants, before making the switch to cricket coaching.

Andy is an ECB Level 3 coach (2006) and is also a member of the Northamptonshire ECB Coach Education team. He is part of the junior coaching set-up at Northants, having coached most age groups, both boys and girls. He is currently coach of the new U-18 boys squad, having coached the U-17 boys team during their ECB National Championship three-day and one-day cup-winning seasons of 2017 and 2019. Andy was head coach of the Northants women's squad, the Steelettos, for eight seasons and headed up the Northants Girls Emerging Players

Programme (EPP), whilst also working on the boys academy and EPP coaching teams. He was also head coach at the Moulton College Cricket Academy for five years, one of the students being Olly Stone (Northants, Warwickshire & England), with others moving on to MCCU cricket.

Andy has been a coach at Stowe School for the past five years, seeing some cricketers progress to MCCU and county 2nd XI cricket. In 2010, Andy was voted National Chance to Shine MCC Spirit of Cricket Coach of the Year.

James and Andrew have over 50 years coaching experience between them. Around their current work commitments they have set up a cricket coaching business (Cricket Coaching Masterclass) offering expert coaching with the overall aim of providing a high quality and enjoyable coaching experience that is player centred and inspires players with a lifelong desire to keep learning and improving. They run specialist courses, masterclasses and one-to-one coaching. To find out more and to contact James & Andy please go through their website: www.cricketcoachingmasterclass.co.uk

CRICKET COACHING MASTERCLASS

ABOUT THE PLAYERS & COACHES

ADAM KING

Adam is the wicketkeeper used in the photos of this book. He is currently at Loughborough University, studying business. He is part of their MCCU and also plays for Northants 2nd XI. Adam has also represented the Midlands in the ECB Super 4s U-17 competition, as well as Buckinghamshire CCC. Adam is a former head boy of Stowe School.

BEN CODDINGTON

Ben is the batsman used in the photos of this book. He is part of the Loughborough MCCU and also plays for Northants 2nd XI and Lincolnshire CCC.

JACK RUSSELL

Jack Russell played 94 matches for England, scoring over 2,000 runs and completing over 200 dismissals behind the stumps. He was considered the best wicketkeeper of his generation. Immaculate glovework – particularly when stood up to the wicket to the seam bowlers – combined with gutsy and determined batting, brought him success both at international level and with his county Gloucestershire.

BEN DUCKETT

Ben Duckett's youth cricket saw him play as a batsman/wicketkeeper for Northamptonshire CCC and Stowe School. Once signed professionally, Ben kept less regularly and began to focus more on his batting. He had incredible success early in his career, with 2016 being his best season to date. That year he scored over 1,300 first-class runs and won the T20 Blast with Northants. This led to him being named as the young cricketer of the year by both the Cricket Writers' Club and the Professional Cricketers' Association (PCA). He was also named PCA Player of the Year – the first player to win both PCA awards in the same season. To date, Ben has played four Test matches, three ODIs and one T20 for England.

DAVID RIPLEY

Following a highly successful 17-year career as Northamptonshire's wicketkeeper, David Ripley moved into coaching. After several years in charge of the 2nd XI and academy teams, David was promoted to the 1st XI job in 2012. He led the team to promotion the following year as well as winning the Friends Life T20. Further T20 success followed when they won the NatWest T20 Blast in 2016.

ALEC STEWART

Alec Stewart played over 300 times for England and captained the team in 1998 and 1999. He played 82 of his 133 Test matches as wicketkeeper. Alec was a fine all-rounder and could bat anywhere in the order, but particularly liked to open. He is one of only a few players to captain, open the batting and keep wicket in a Test match. Alec has been Surrey's Director of Cricket since 2013, producing several of the current crop of England international cricketers in that time, including Sam Curran, Tom Curran, Rory Burns, Dominic Sibley, Ben Foakes, Jason Roy and Ollie Pope.

ALAN KNOTT

Alan Knott is regarded as the best wicketkeeper of his generation, playing 95 Test matches and 20 ODIs for England. This would have been more if not for bans he received for taking part in World Series Cricket and a rebel tour to South Africa. In 2009, Knott was inducted into the ICC Hall of Fame and in 2013 was named as the wicketkeeper in Wisden's all-time Test World XI. After retiring from professional cricket in 1985, he coached England's wicketkeepers, as well as being an assessor for the England side.

TOM MOORES

Tom Moores is the current wicketkeeper/batsman at Nottinghamshire County Cricket Club. He has found great success in their limited-overs teams, in particular as a highly competent wicketkeeper and powerful middle-order batsman.

PETER MOORES

After a long playing career with Sussex and Worcestershire, Peter Moores has had great success as a coach both at county and international level. He has had two spells in charge of the England team as their head coach and is the only coach to have won the county championship with two different counties – Sussex and Lancashire. Peter is now a coach with Nottinghamshire County Cricket Club.

ACKNOWLEDGEMENTS

Firstly, we have to thank the many players and coaches who gave up their time and their knowledge to contribute to this book – Alan Knott, Jack Russell, Alec Stewart, Peter Moores, Tom Moores, David Ripley and Ben Duckett. They were very giving and generous with their time and we are extremely grateful to them all. Also, to Adam King and Ben Coddington who spent several days in cricket gear whilst the photographs were taken. Special thanks goes to Jonathan Glynn-Smith and Leah Band @StoweStudio100 for their hard work taking such high quality photos over the three day shoot, and then the several days further enhancing the images you see in this book.

A thank you to the Stowe School Headmaster – Dr Anthony Wallersteiner – who allowed us to use the Stowe School Cricket facilities for the photographs. Also, to Steve Curley – the Head Groundsman – and his team of groundstaff who were out at 7 a.m. each morning preparing the grounds and nets prior to each days photoshoot. As novices to the publishing world we are very grateful to our agent, David Luxton, whose support and advice was invaluable and persuaded Polaris Publishing to invest in us. Thank you to Peter Burns and his team at Polaris for their help in developing the book.

We would also like to thank all of those who have helped us both on our cricketing journey throughout the years that led us to this point: our families, our friends, our teammates, our co-workers, other teachers and other coaches. They have all inspired, encouraged, challenged, and shared their knowledge and experiences with us over many years and, without that, this book would never have been written.

Lastly, a huge thank you to you the reader for buying this book. We very much hope you enjoy it and, whether a player or coach, that it helps you out on your own cricketing journey.

Andrew O'Connor   James Knott